HOW TO MAKE

Good pictures

A guide for the amateur photographer

Eastman Kodak Company • Rochester, New York

Contents

What this book is all about

THIS new edition of *How To Make Good Pictures* has but one purpose—to help you get the most enjoyment, and the most satisfying results, from your camera.

It's a book for everybody. Maybe you're a grandparent . . . maybe a grade school student, a high school junior, a proud new mother, a busy professional man seeking an interesting and creative hobby. Whatever your age or interests, picture taking has much to offer you — and this book provides a basic guide.

the aim: to help you see

The book's approach is simple: to help you see the picture possibilities that exist all around you, and then to help you make the most of these possibilities, through wise choice of viewpoint, lighting, good subject arrangement, and correct operation of your camera.

This book is definitely *not* a collection of professional photographs. Most of the pictures were made by amateur photographers, with amateur cameras. ("Amateur," by the way, does not mean "dub"; it is a proud word, signifying one who takes pictures for the love of it, rather than as a means of livelihood.) The pictures are good because they represent the honest, sympathetic observation of people who have learned to *see* their surroundings — and to record their pleasure accurately on photographic film.

3

here's the general outline

The first section, "Let's Make a Picture" is a running account of the steps taken in making a typical snapshot with typical snapshot equipment. It points out pitfalls — and how to side-step them. It shows that there may be (there usually are) dozens of ways to make good pictures from any one situation.

Then, having covered some of the basic business of making a good snapshot, there's a bit of talk about how cameras work, how cameras differ, why there are several types of film, and how to pick out a camera suited to your requirements. Color is taken "in stride," for practically every camera today is a color camera.

what, where, when — and how

In Part Two there's a good deal of information about specific picture-making projects — under widely various conditions. It is, of course, not quite possible to cover in detail every single kind of picture you might want to make, but a little cross reference among the several circumstances that *are* detailed should give you what you need.

Part Three goes into the darkroom to brief you on the processes of developing, printing, enlarging, and a number of other operations. Part Four provides some indication of the many ways you can use the pictures your camera and your darkroom work have produced.

If you're like most of us, you learn best by doing. So we'll start right off with making a picture.

> ✔ A word to the wise. This book contains a great deal of useful information — too much to digest in one lump. The next three chapters will get you off to a good start; read them carefully. Then, beginning with Page 39, skim through the rest of the book, to obtain a quick survey of amateur photography and the wonderful opportunities it offers you. Finally, come back to Page 39, and resume your careful study. Pay special attention to the chapters on "Choosing your equipment" and "Pictures in full color" — they contain technical facts and advice that are most helpful in all your picture taking.

Let's make a picture

THIS CHAPTER begins where your camera manual ends.

The manual tells you how to load film, set the shutter, use the view finder—in short, the *mechanical* details of camera operation. With that information alone, you can make sharp, correctly exposed snapshots under average conditions.

But will they be *good pictures?*

Quite often, they will. You've heard of beginner's luck. Yet now and then, you'll find yourself frowning at a picture that should have been very good—and wondering just what went wrong.

In ninety-nine cases out of a hundred, an experienced taker of good pictures could spot your difficulty at a glance. He'd point out a background . . . incorrect lighting . . . or one of several other common, easily avoided errors.

Your experienced camera fan evades such errors through a simple, step-by-step technique. Let's watch him closely as he tackles a typical snapshot subject—a small girl, receiving a new doll from her father.

first, he defines the picture idea . . .

In this case, simply the presentation of the doll, but emphasizing the child's delight in the gift.

and he limits the subject matter . . .

Father, doll, child, and a simple home background against

which the action will stand out clearly. Anything more is un-desirable—because it would complicate the scene, and draw attention away from the subjects.

now, he picks out a location . . .

Shooting from the doorway of the house obviously won't do in this case. Sun is in wrong position.

Shooting from sidewalk, the tree and house make a busy, jumbled background.

However, he notes th the house front is in sha ow, with sun on the fro step. The shaded doorw will make a good bac ground; the sunny step an ideal spot to place t child.

next, the camera distance . . .

Evidently, this is too far back; the picture would be all house, no people.

The close-up is better (and even simple, non-focusing cameras can make them).

An extreme close-up wi the camera held very hig offers a novel angle.

finally, the camera elevation . . .

Low viewpoint (with camera held low) would be nearer the child's eye level.

Higher camera position usually shows action more clearly.

Very high viewpoint (with camera overhead) offers a bird's-eye-view — sometimes very useful.

and the best left-to-right position . . .

Straight front position might show the action nicely, but the setting would be rather dull.

Position to right of walk would show sunny side of subjects, while the diagonal view of the doorway offers prospect of more pleasing pictures.

The expert's choice in this case would, most likely, be to the right of the walk, six to eight feet from the doorway, with camera at waist level (ready to move up or down at need). Then, with the lighting, location, and viewpoint neatly worked out, he'd be ready for a delightful picture series (next page).

7

the expert never takes "just one shot"

Every experienced photographer knows that a good subject
or situation holds many good pictures. When it's an "action
situation" such as this, opportunity is ideal for a picture series.
And with an easy-to-handle camera such as the Kodak Duaflex
Camera—plus wise choice of the camera position—the series
isn't difficult to take. Here's what experience gives you . . . . .

4

5

6

"Oh, stop teasing!"
Camera has been low-
ered here, and bush in
foreground is obscuring
the child. Higher view-
point is preferable; note
the preceding pictures.

"Ooooh!"
Action is seen in pro-
file, so it is clear and
self-explanatory. The
picture tells its story
simply and quickly—as
every good picture
must do.

"What will I call her
Viewpoint has be
changed a step to t
left, and camera
nearer the subjec
This not only mak
them larger, but a
simplifies the scene.

here's the camera
The Kodak Duaflex Camera used to take all these
pictures is a simple, moderately-priced beginner's
type. You can take good pictures with *any* Kodak
or Brownie Camera. Actual size of Kodak Duaflex
Camera negatives is 2¼ x 2¼ inches; standard oversize prints and Kodacolor Prints are 3½ x 3½ inches.

8

2

3

"Wonder what it is"

Study the setting here—background is uniformly shaded, but subject is in sunshine. This assures simplicity and good contrast. Camera is a step too far from subject.

"Must be something nice"

Here again, note the importance of showing light-colored subjects against a dark background. Dark subjects are usually best against a light or medium-toned background.

"Did you bring it?"

In picturing children, watch the hands—they're fully as expressive as the face. Note that the camera has moved nearer; this is just about the right distance.

8

9

"Thank you so much"

Viewpoint is still more to the front here, and camera still closer. View of the child's expression is better. Father's feet are cut off, but it doesn't matter; the child is the center of interest.

"You're wonderful"

Faces are practically hidden here, but the action is clear—partly because of the preceding pictures. Camera was aimed a little too far to the right.

"You hold her while I look"

Nine good album pictures from one simple situation! Note return to original viewpoint here, with camera high and to the right.

now let's look at some fumbles

PRACTICALLY all the preceding pictures are good; not works of art, of course, but clear, attractive album shots. Now let's take a quick look at some of the common camera mistakes—and how to avoid them. That will about complete your "basic training."

Underexposure

This is a snapshot of subjects in deep shade, under a tree. Poor details; not enough light. For snaps in the shade, use synchronized photoflash (see Page 50).

Tilted Camera

Result of not observing carefully enough through the view finder, right up through the moment of release. Keep your eye on the subject, through the view finder, until *after* the shutter clicks!

Overexposure

This is a print from a too-long exposure taken in bright sunlight. Details are chalky, "burned up." It happens with simple cameras if you make a "time" or "bulb" exposure in sunshine.

Camera Movement

The whole picture is blurred. It happens when you "punch" the shutter release. Always stand steady, hold your breath, and release the shutter gently. Your subject won't run away.

Double Exposure

Two pictures accidentally taken on one film; a pretty poor way to make film go farther. It won't happen if you wind the film *immediately* after taking each picture.

10

Bad Lighting

Facing squarely into the sun usually means squinting, hard shadows, hollow eye-sockets. Noon isn't the best time for outdoor pictures; forenoon and afternoon are better, with the sun a little to one side so it doesn't glare into the subject's eyes.

Dirty Lens

You can't see through your glasses when the lenses are dirty. A camera can't "see" either, when its lens is soiled. Use lens tissue and lens cleaner, and keep the lens spotless; it pays.

Subject Partly Cut Off

This is merely another case of careless view-finding. Keep your eye on the finder image and keep the subject accurately framed until after the shutter clicks.

Bad Background

Action is lost against the tree. Always look beyond the subject before you shoot; if the background is bad, change your camera position, or move the subject, or both.

Subject Out of Focus

With simple cameras, it happens when you bring the camera too near the subject. For real close-ups with such cameras, put a Kodak Close-up Attachment over the camera lens.

Lens Obscured

Usually, it's a finger in front of the lens; in this case, it's the camera neckstrap. Just learn to handle your camera so your fingers, or the strap, don't get out in front.

11

Good and better pictures

WHAT IS IT that lifts a picture out of the "just average" class, and puts it in top rank?

What are the subtle elements of appeal that make people exclaim over a picture, and then follow their exclamation with those sweetest of all words, "You mean you took this picture *yourself?*"

In this chapter, we'll try to answer those questions, at least in part, by comparing a number of good and better pictures, and analyzing the features that make them successful.

be critical as you go along

Perhaps you won't agree with all the comments. Perhaps you can think of ways in which some of the "better" pictures might be made better still. If so, that's all to the good; it means you're developing your critical judgment, and sharpening up your "picture eye." But don't stop with mere criticism; load up your camera, seek out a suitable subject, and *test your views in practice*. The proof of the pudding is in the print.

Truth is, few persons agree on every tiny detail of a fine picture. It's not necessary that they should. The important thing is to develop a keen judgment for subject matter, lighting, arrangement, and viewpoint. Then, if you like a picture, it's a good picture. If *everybody* likes it, the picture deserves to go in Class A.

NONE BETTER Here's a human-interest masterpiece — snapped by an amateur, with an amateur camera. Study it carefully. Note there's no "camera consciousness"; everybody's absorbed in the job. Next, the grouping; all four figures are combined in a clear, well-organized unit. (Good selection of viewpoint did that; a camera position farther to left or right, or lower down, would have hurt the picture.) Finally, see how the picture was snapped at the perfect moment to capture each child's personality: the master mechanic, the critic, the skeptic, the let-me-show-you-how supervisor at left. You can't pose or plan such situations — but keep your eyes open, and you'll find them in every neighborhood in the U.S.

13

◀ GOOD Because the action is good, the bride watching her step, the groom in full stride, his face squinched up as he waits for a shower of rice . . . they're nicely framed by the crowd and the simple dark background . . . all in all, a clear, straightforward, honest picture, snapped at the right moment, with no posing — and full of good fun.

BETTER Because of its explosive spontaneity . . . the vigorous action, storms of rice, waving hands — even the slight tilt of the camera! Ordinarily, accidental tilting of a camera harms the picture — but in this one, the slight tilt actually helps intensify the exciting, catch-as-catch-can feeling. Judged on "technical" grounds, this isn't as good a photograph as the one above — it's not as sharp, not as clear — but as a *picture*, an effective record of a riotous moment, it's far ahead. If you were the editor of a picture magazine, and had to choose between the two — you'd pick this one instantly, and probably print it full page. ▶

points to remember

✔ Spontaneity—the feeling that here's a natural moment with all its natural flavor — is the most important element in a snapshot. If a picture looks posed—well, it looks posed. What worse thing could you say about it?

✔ You need not show all of a person — especially if he's not the main subject. In the pictures above, the crowd is mostly cut off — a face here, a hand there, or part of a figure. That's as it should be, because in these pictures the emphasis belongs on the bride and groom.

✔ It takes a fast shutter to "stop" fast action. However, you don't need to freeze all action dead cold; sometimes a blurred detail is helpful. Note the rice and the blurred hand above; they make the picture better. But this applies only in pictures of fast action — not to still or slow-moving subjects.

✔ A simple, contrasting background — either lighter or darker than your subject — always helps a picture.

◀ **GOOD** Because it's simple in plan . . . close up . . . clear, with an excellent plain background and foreground . . . but above all, because of the expression and the eye, emphasized by lighting, with its large pendent teardrop.

GOOD Because of its simplicity, excellent contrast between head and background, and a foreground which leads you right up to the big peeping eyes. Good, too, because of the interesting lighting and viewpoint—both down lower than usual, and therefore distinctive. These two pictures emphasize the value of a close-up lens. At close range, it's easier to keep things simple — to eliminate extraneous material — and to give your small subject the emphasis he should have in your picture. ▶

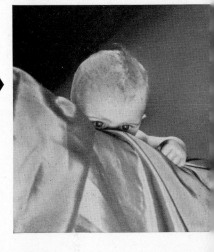

◀ **GOOD** Because it tells its story directly, clearly, without effort . . . because it's simple, restricted to the essentials . . . because it's natural, spontaneous, and expressive, full of the mother's glowing pride in her new, sleepy child.

GOOD Because of its clarity . . . naturalness . . . pleasant grouping, simple lighting, and contrasting background. Note how the dark background "holds the picture together"—and how the mother's glance leads you to the baby's face. ▶

15

people

GOOD —because she's an attractive subject, nicely placed with her side to the sun, to avoid eyestrain and squinting. The camera was low, to obtain a simple uncluttered background of sky; and a color filter helped deepen the sky tone. The rough wooden rail provides an adequate "base" for the picture, and unobtrusively suggests a pleasant rustic location. Best of all, the whole feeling of the picture is natural and casual, with no attempt at elaborate posing or forced animation.

BETTER —even though the sun is too nearly straight overhead for perfect "portrait" lighting. The subject's position is pleasant, relaxed, natural. Again, the camera is low, for a sky background, with a filter to deepen the sky tone. This provides better contrast with the white dress. Trees at lower left and right lend desirable "weight" at the base of the picture; and the rail crosses at an attractive diagonal—far better than a dull horizontal arrangement. Note also that the girl's body makes a diagonal — unlike the straight up-and-down pose above. Clouds nicely break up the sky areas — avoiding monotony.

points to remember

Every rule in portraiture has its exceptions, but these usually hold true:

✔ Keep the background simple. Outdoors, the sky is one of the best backgrounds. A color filter (K-2 or X-1) helps assure pleasing tone values in the sky.

✔ For an effect of candor, let your subject look directly at the camera; for a dreamy or detached effect, let the subject look beyond the camera.

✔ Don't center your subject. The picture at the top of this page would be better if trimmed or "cropped" at the right. Block off half an inch, and see for yourself. In your first pictures, try placing the subject's head about halfway between the center and one corner, as in the picture above. And don't crowd the subject's head against the top of the picture; leave enough room for comfort.

✔ Sunshine lends sparkle to an outdoor portrait — but keep the sun out of your subject's eyes.

✔ Avoid noon sun. Mid-morning or mid-afternoon sun tends to give a pleasing 45-degree lighting.

16

GOOD — because it's clear, sharp, pleasantly back-lighted, and quite natural. The child's casual dress is set off nicely by the massive background. Try blocking off part of the background, to improve the position of the subject in the picture space. (You can do it with the view finder when taking pictures.)

BETTER — because it tells a story. In many details, it's just like the picture above, with a small girl, outdoor location, back lighting, and so on. But that coy eye, peeking out over the newspaper, makes all the difference. Your imagination supplies the boy friend with the ice cream cone.

points to remember

↙Pictures are more interesting when they tell a story. And all it takes is a subject doing something . . . doing almost anything! Make a list of small everyday events — a boy putting on his skates, a pup greeting a kitten, Dad putting cream in his coffee. Make it as long as you like — and you'll find a "story" picture in every item! Never forget this, because it's the basic secret of interesting snapshots.

↙ Back lighting and "open shade" are very pleasant for pictures of children — and adults with blonde hair. Give about twice the normal direct-sunshine exposure (for example, with Kodak Veri- chrome Film, give 1/50 second at $f/8$ instead of 1/50 at $f/11$).

17

GOOD — because the subject is nice, the expression good, the toy is appropriate, the color scheme is simple (and there are no spots of intense, demanding color to draw your eye away from the child's face). It would be a better picture if the background were darker or in deep shadow; the pattern of the bricks is too emphatic — like a piano accompaniment so loud you can't hear the singer. Note the softness of the lighting — it's almost "flat," with just enough shadow to bring out the modeling of the face. An extra light was used behind the child to highlight the hair.

BETTER — because it tells a story, the background has no pattern (although it is rather overwhelming in brightness of color), the expression and action are good, the pose is charming, and accents of red are nicely placed. If you like bright hues, you'll prefer the color scheme in this one; if you lean to subdued colors, you'll prefer the facing picture. (Incidentally, the subject didn't blow those bubbles; they were blown in by a helper, and as soon as the photographer sensed a pleasing pattern, he snapped it.)

19

hands

GOOD ◀ — because it's clear and sharp, the hands are shown in action, the crocheting is clearly delineated against a dark background. (Here's one case where pattern is desirable — because it's an essential part of the "picture story.") Hands are immensely expressive; make many close-ups of them.

BETTER — because the action is more interesting the design is informal (not symmetrical, like the picture above); the lighting brings out the form and character of the hands; the crocheting falls in interesting folds, with variation of light and shade; the dark dress provides a more meaningful background, and the dark all-around frame helps concentrate interest on the hands and needlework. You can learn a great deal about picture arrangement, through a point-by-point study of these two pictures. ▶

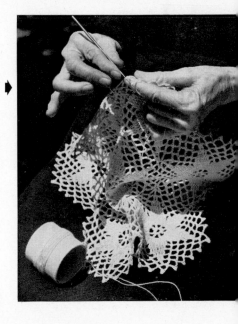

flowers

GOOD — because the hour was well chosen for good lighting, the camera was held low for a background of sky, and a filter was used. ▼

BETTER — because the flowers are dramatically back-lighted, and the curve of the stems lends an interesting, eye-catching rhythm. Low camera, filtered sky. ▼

GOOD — because it's extremely simple, neatly arranged, with a good pose and good expression in the subjects. It wouldn't be nearly as good if both heads were at exactly the same level. Would you center the heads like this? — or trim away some background at left and top? — or all around? Try various croppings, to see which you prefer.

GOOD — because it's simple and clear, with interesting lighting and an unusual camera angle. This is a picture that almost tells a story—but doesn't quite make it. If the cat appeared agitated, excited — then your mind would fill in the "story" plot.

GOOD — because it is perfectly true to type; cats like to stalk, and to peer over and around things. Note how the shadow contributes to the effect. Compare this with the second baby picture on Page 15; both derive their interest from the eyes.

GOOD — because the action, the cat's bristling tail and challenging expression, and the china dog's bored indifference, suggest a story theme. It's the type of shot that brings a chuckle whenever you see it. With less pattern in the background, it would be more effective.

BETTER — because it has everything a "story picture" needs — simplicity, directness, no distractions, clear arrangement, and an ideally doleful expression in the freshly-laundered pup.

21

GOOD — because of the intent expressions, the interesting stepped-down pose of the dogs' heads, and the novel framing. This is a picture which would be quite as good in black-and-white, because there's practically no color in the subject matter. It was chosen deliberately for contrast with the colorful snap below.

BETTER — as a color subject. In this shot, color makes an important contribution; the delicate color of the puppy's coat, and many other details, gain added realism on Kodachrome Film. Large area of background is helpful here, to accent the smallness of the pup; block away part of it, and see.

study these lightings; which do you prefer?

Front lighting. No deep shadows.

Top lighting. "Noon sun." Hard shadows.

Back lighting; reflector facing subject.

Open shade. Very soft, no shadows.

GOOD —because it tells a story; the action is clear and self-explanatory; grouping of the subjects is excellent; and the camera position was properly chosen to convey the story.

BETTER —because it is simpler and more direct, telling the same story as above with fewer details and livelier action. Note how the shadows outline the boy and basket, very clearly and strongly. Note also that the boy's feet are spread, and he's leaning forward a bit — while the girl above is standing perfectly straight. This more active stance gives the large picture a better feeling of life and movement. Always seek simplicity, directness, and the feel of action.

GOOD — because the story is there, even though it's as simple as a small girl mocking the bleating of a lamb . . . and because the low camera neatly outlines the action against the sky.

GOOD — because the story is told with crystal clarity against a background smartly chosen to set off every detail.

◀ GOOD — because it's natural, with no sense of "posing"... the action is good, the children well placed and clearly separated ... the curving wall lends a graceful touch ... the lighting is pleasant, both on the figures and on the simple background of rippling water.

BETTER — because, although the figures are in about the same relationship as those above, they're a little better placed ... the lighting is more dramatic, and the light and dark areas are more effectively grouped ... the figures stand out more clearly against a perfectly simple background (note, above, that the little girl's head tends to merge into the distant foliage) ... and the story is more interesting, with the small boat going off on a cruise of its own. This picture, by the way, was made by a high school student, and won one of the top prizes in a national photographic competition. It is worth careful study. Note that while it's a back view, there's plenty of expression in the figures — the faces aren't needed!

points to remember

✓ There are no substitutes for simplicity and clear action. Pick out the two or three pictures you like best on these two pages — and you'll find you have chosen the ones with the least detail, and with action standing out clearly against a simple background.

✓ To draw the eye to a certain point or object, place the object against a background of the strongest contrasting tone. Note the milk bottle on Page 24, and the basket in the boy's hands. They are the details you see first.

✓ If a person in the picture is looking at something, your eye will be drawn there too. You can test this effect with every picture on these two pages.

✓ Diagonal lines are "lines of action"— they tend to breathe life into a picture. Note the feeling of a diagonal arrangement in the picture above; and in the large picture on the facing page, note that the boy's leg, the basket, and the horse's head make a rough diagonal from the bottom right corner of the picture to the upper left corner.

◀ **GOOD** — because it caught the jumper in mid-air, with a bit of the crowd at each side, and the valley beyond and below. But the jumper looks too much as if he's pasted against the far hill!

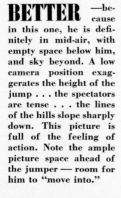

BETTER —because in this one, he is definitely in mid-air, with empty space below him, and sky beyond. A low camera position exaggerates the height of the jump . . . the spectators are tense . . . the lines of the hills slope sharply down. This picture is full of the feeling of action. Note the ample picture space ahead of the jumper — room for him to "move into." ▶

◀ **GOOD** — because the background is drawn out into a long blur, but the boat is sharp. This creates a sense of great speed. Picture was taken with a box camera, using the "panoram" method — swinging the camera to keep the subject centered in the view finder, and snapping the picture "in stride." This technique works for pictures of automobiles, too.

GOOD — because the high camera position, ▶ and the diagonal wake of the boat, create an excellent sense of fast motion — which is usually the very essence of an effective sports picture.

26

◀ **GOOD** — as a story picture of a favorite artists' haunt. It's a nicely arranged picture, too; the dark float in the foreground, placed to right of center, balances the dark mass of buildings and shadow at the upper left. The "story" would be better without the boat and fisherman beyond the artist's easel; they interfere. A lower camera position, nearer to the artist, might have helped "tell the story" better.

GOOD — as a straightforward scenic view of the same location. Note that this is the material the artist, pictured above, has selected for his painting.

points to remember

✔ Before taking a picture, define your purpose. Is it to be a "story" picture, a scenic or pictorial study, or what? What do you want the picture to say?

✔ In choosing and arranging picture material (especially scenics) always try for pictorial balance — a "balancing of masses." Here's what that means. Imagine the scene above to be suspended from a hook in its center — the roofpeak of the second house. Now, observe how the dark wedge of shadow, on the right, balances against the dark house on the left. In every picture that appeals to you because of its beauty, you will find lines and masses which tend to create a balanced design, a pictorial equilibrium.

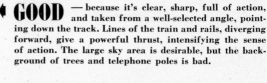

◀ **GOOD** — because it's clear, sharp, full of action, and taken from a well-selected angle, pointing down the track. Lines of the train and rails, diverging forward, give a powerful thrust, intensifying the sense of action. The large sky area is desirable, but the background of trees and telephone poles is bad.

BETTER — f o r here the background is clear of detail, so the engine stands out sharply . . . and the crisp contrast of white smoke against dark shadow, and dark rails against white stone, lend snap and sparkle. There's good action in every line of this picture — and the low viewpoint adds extra drama. ▶

◀ **BEST** — because of its atmospheric quality, the interesting pattern of steam and smoke, and the pattern of curving rails. High viewpoint was best here. This picture has pictorial and emotional qualities the others lack — beauty as well as dramatic action.

points to remember

✓ Don't let a horizon line cut your pictures in half. Keep it above or below the middle, as in all the pictures on these two pages.

✓ Curved lines lend grace to a picture; diagonal lines tend to be exciting and active; powerful contrasts of size, as on the facing page, tend to add drama and human interest.

✓ Atmospheric quality — smoke, haze, fog — will often inject emotional appeal into the most ordinary scenes. In distant views, haze intensifies the feeling of distance — adds depth and "third dimension."

◀ **GOOD** — because it's a natural moment, captured in a natural manner, without fuss or fanfare. Children admiring aircraft are always good human-interest material.

BETTER — because of the dramatic contrast between the small, enraptured boy, and the huge, powerful airplane. The low camera position is important here — it lifts the plane up against the sky, emphasizing its size.

▼

◀ **GOOD** — as a clear, sharp record picture of the home town band. The important thing in such snaps is identification; if you can pick out all the people you know, the picture is successful. A higher camera position (on top of a car, for example) would have helped clear the background. Color helps too; compare the band on Page 205.

GOOD — as a dramatic pictorial study of a parading band. In this one, the general pattern is more important than the individual members. Note the high viewpoint . . . skillful use of the diagonal line of the street, to create action and movement . . . good balancing of the dark foreground and the shadowed building across the street . . . and the precise timing, with the band and colors in exactly the right position to complete the design of the picture. Obviously, the maker of this picture did some brainwork ahead of time — and chose his viewpoint to fit a plan he'd worked out in his mind.

points to remember

✔ To show groups of people in action, a high viewpoint is generally best. This applies especially to sports action — games between teams, and the like. When you're high up, the action spreads out below you like a map — and your pictures clearly reveal what was happening.

✔ When a background bothers you, try a change in camera position — to left or right, higher up or lower down. Watch for "mergers" — such as the tree or telephone post that always wants to stick up right back of your subject.

✔ Keep the design simple. Just for fun, lay a piece of tracing paper over the larger picture above, and shade the dark areas with a soft pencil. You'll find only three elements in the picture — two irregular masses of shadow, and a broad diagonal line between. That's why the picture has so much force.

30

GOOD —because the dark lamp standards resemble sentinels, standing guard over the silent, deserted street, with the city beyond half lost in dusk and fog. It's a type of picture that gives your imagination something to work on.

BETTER —because the human element has been introduced . . . because the dark buildings are more effectively massed, and punctuated by twinkling points of light . . . because the tonal gradation of the buildings, from dark to middletone to pale, lends depth and distance . . . because the man and boy are strongly silhouetted against a light area . . . because the umbrella and streets gleam with moisture. This evening is so wet you can feel it in your bones. Get out your raincoat; the worse the weather becomes, the better it is for taking pictures with true atmospheric appeal. And with modern fast films, plus modern fast lenses, bad weather is no fatal obstacle.

points to remember

✔ A "strong" foreground—a prominent shadow, figure, or dark object—accents the feeling of depth or distance in a picture. It adds "third dimension."

✔ A dark object against a light area, or a bright object against a dark area, helps create a "center of interest." It attracts your eye; and the stronger the contrast, the stronger the attraction. Artists speak of "placing the brightest highlight against the deepest shadow"— as the best way to force the observer's attention just where they want it to go.

✔ Foreground figures commonly help a scenic picture, city or rural. They should look at the scene, not at the camera.

✔ Usually, the most important object in a picture should be placed about halfway between the center of the picture and one corner. Note the placing of the heads and umbrella, in the picture above.

31

GOOD — as a well-planned record picture of a public building in its holiday dress. The time exposure was just long enough to bring out the building detail. Viewpoint was properly chosen to place the Christmas tree at one side, so it does not blot out the building.

BETTER — as a dramatic pictorial illustration. Observe how carefully the maker selected his camera height and position, so as to line up the horseman against the brilliantly lighted tower. The strong, clearly outlined statues, with the bright building as a backdrop, make a very simple, very forceful picture design. You can take such pictures with any camera that has a "T" or "B" setting for "time exposures."

points to remember

🗸 Unusual lighting effects are nearly always interesting, and large areas of deep rich black have great pictorial strength. These two things help account for the appeal of most outdoor pictures taken at night.

🗸 Silhouettes—black against white, without detail in the black—are also pictorially "strong," full of impact. However, a silhouetted figure must be posed properly — usually in profile — so the outline clearly portrays all the action you want to show.

🗸 Once again: define your picture idea before you shoot. Decide what type of picture you're seeking — what you want it to say. (The pictures above are of the same building — but one is a seasonal record; the other, a pictorial study arranged for dramatic effect.)

32

What is photography?

Up to now, we've stayed away from theory, and concentrated on pictures — which are a lot more fun. However, if you plan to be a first-class amateur photographer, you need to know a few underlying fundamentals of photography.

With a camera, you can make pictures of almost anything you can see. A bit of a miracle, that. And it depends on one simple scientific fact. *Silver can be made sensitive to light.*

Examine a dime or a twenty-five-cent piece. It's silver — nice, shiny silver. Now, examine the black image in one of your film negatives. That's silver too; it's black because it consists of finely-divided rough particles.

When you bought that film, unexposed, the silver was in a different form. It existed as whitish silver salts — silver "halides." They had been treated with sensitizing dyes, heated, mixed with gelatin, finally coated on a transparent film base, dried, and packed in a light-tight roll or box.

Then you loaded the film into your camera—aimed the camera at a scene—and pressed the button. The camera shutter opened. Light passed through. The lens focused an image on the light-sensitive film, which had never seen light before. And an invisible, "latent" image was formed, wherever sufficient light touched the sensitive silver-salt emulsion of the film.

In due time, your photofinisher immersed the film in a developing solution. Quickly, the light-struck silver salts turned into particles of black metallic silver. A "fixing bath" dissolved out the silver salts that had *not* been affected by light—and there was your negative, complete in every detail.

But — it was in reverse. Everything that should be white was black. So, as a last step, your photofinisher took a piece of sensitized paper — coated with silver salts just about like the film — and exposed it to light *through* the negative. In other words, he printed a negative *from* the negative — and, as in grammar, the negative of a photographic negative is a positive.

So, after development, there was your positive print — an album print on paper, ready for viewing.

And that, in a nutshell, is photography—the process of making pictures by means of light.

no light, no photographs

Light is the great essential. Always remember that. No photograph has ever been made without light. You may read of pictures snapped "in absolute darkness"— but they were actually taken by means of infrared or ultraviolet light, which the human eye cannot see.

Wherever there is visible or invisible light, you can take pictures—if you have the right camera and the right film. Your light

34   may be sunlight, moonlight, or starlight; a feeble candle, a kero-

An ordinary match is the sole light source in this picture. ➔

← All the light for this snapshot came from the sparklers. Fast film, 1/25 second at *f*/2.9.

Candles and a match provide the only light here. A 3-second exposure at *f*/3.5. ➔

⬅ Fast film,
1/200 at
f/3.5.

By theater
spotlight, ➡
1/25, f/4.5.

sene lamp, an electric arc or spark, or even an electric iron heated to the point where it emits infrared rays. It may be a theater spotlight, a photoflood lamp, a photoflash lamp. Any of these sources can be — and has been — used to take pictures; the basic difference is that some sources permit exposures measured in millionths of a second, while certain others require exposures measured in minutes or hours.

With the right equipment, the size and speed of a subject hardly matter. You can take a snapshot of a mountain range, then put your camera on a microscope and take pictures of microbes — all on the same roll of film! With ultra-speed electronic flash equipment, scientists can picture motion that is too fast for the eye to see—such as the impact of a golf club against the ball, or the flight of a bullet from a gun.

A fine camera is a marvelous instrument, and easy to use, once you have learned the purpose of its several parts. But you must always remember that it does not have a mind of its own. It faithfully pictures just what *you* put in front of it. So, the final responsibility for good pictures—and the credit for them—rests right on you.

Pages 36-37 illustrate the basic features of a good camera, and how they serve to regulate and control the light that makes the picture. Each of these camera elements is analyzed in more detail in Chapter 6, "Choosing Your Equipment."

Inside a camera

 1. This small character is a photon, a unit of light. He and his innumerable brothers move in straight lines at 186,000 miles a second.

2. When light units hit something, they bounce back — or are absorbed. If they bounce back to your eye, the object looks bright . . . If they are absorbed, the object looks dark.

3. From every bright part of a scene, many units of light radiate to the lens of your camera — and the lens lines them up and passes each unit along to the proper point on the film.

4. A large-aperture lens cannot focus sharply the light units from both very near and very far objects. Therefore, it's mounted so it can be moved forward or back, until it's set for the objects you want sharpest.

5. The film at the back of your camera is a sensitive silver screen. Units of light strike it and leave an invisible record, a "latent image." Each unit, sent to its proper spot by the lens, adds a little to the pattern of light — thus reproducing the scene the lens sees. (Later on, chemical development makes the "latent image" visible.) To measure out exactly the right number of units from the available light, your camera has two "front gates" (see below).

6. Your camera's shutter is a gate which opens and closes quickly (unless you've set it for "bulb" or "time" exposures). When it's shut, no light passes through. The shutter (below) always opens fully and closes completely. But the other gate (the diaphragm, on facing page) is always partly open or wide open, to admit more or fewer units of light.

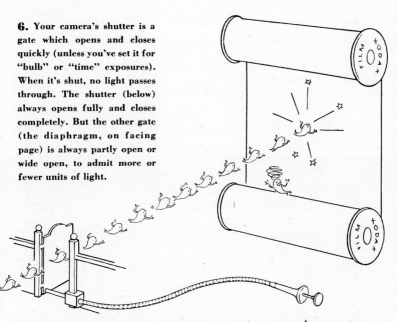

7. When the light is strong, as in bright sun, many units can crowd quickly through the shutter. But when light is dim, with units scattered and few the shutter must remain open longer, so enough units can straggle through and impress the picture image on the film.

8. Instead of leaving the shutter open longer, you can open the camera's other "front gate"— the lens diaphragm — to a wider setting. The wider it's open, the more light passes through in a given time. In dim light, a wide-open lens setting may permit you to take snapshots at 1/25 or 1/50 second, instead of making "time" exposures. In bright light, you may often close your diaphragm down to a small opening — such as $f/11$ or $f/16$ — and your lens will then focus a deeper zone, helping you get both near and far objects sharp. The reserve lens speed, adjustable diaphragm, focusing movement, and shutter with a choice of speeds, all enlarge the picture capacity of a fine camera.

Camera care

it pays big dividends

As YOU'LL learn in the next chapter, a camera is a carefully designed optical instrument — made to give years of reliable service, but not to tolerate abuse. Follow these simple hints, and your new camera will serve you long and well:

✔ Keep your camera in a case to protect it from bumps and bangs. A "field case" of the ever-ready, drop-front type is generally most convenient.

✔ Do NOT keep your camera in the glove compartment of a car — especially when the car is parked in the sun. Heat in a closed compartment often becomes intense enough to cause serious damage.

✔ Keep the lens clean. A drop of Kodak Lens Cleaner, and gentle wiping with soft Kodak Lens Tissue, will leave it crystal-bright. Glance at the lens for dust and fingerprints before you take a picture. On Page 11 you saw what a dirty lens will do.

✔ When loading the camera at a beach, or in dusty places, make sure that grit and sand don't get inside. From time to time, it's wise to dust out the interior of the camera carefully with a soft brush.

✔ Never oil your camera shutter, and never take it apart. If any part of the camera mechanism becomes "balky," don't force it. Let a trained repairman check it and correct the trouble.

✔ Twice a year, take your camera to your Kodak dealer for a routine inspection. A month or so before Christmas, and before your summer vacation, are logical times for these semi-annual checkups.

Choosing
your equipment

THE BEST CAMERA for you is one that will get the pictures you want. It may be you now have a simple fixed-focus camera; and if you use it judiciously, as outlined on Pages 5 through 11, it will serve you well. But if you are interested in sports shots, action subjects under a wide range of light conditions, fine pictorial work, big exhibition enlargements, or color transparencies for screen projection — then you require a camera with faster lens, and a shutter that offers several speeds. The cost is greater, but so is the satisfaction of ownership.

analyze your needs before choosing

Before reading farther, study the chart on the next two pages, and analyze your needs. What are you going to *do* with this camera? Is it for general family use, on non-moving or slow-moving subjects? Are the pictures simply for album use — not for enlargement or exhibition? Are they to be casual snaps, or carefully composed from a pictorial and artistic standpoint? Will you want to capture sports and fast-action subjects? How about flower shots, or nature studies, in full color — and candid shots under difficult light?

Decide these points, and you have the foundation for an intelligent, satisfying choice. From the facts on Pages 40-41, plus additional details your Kodak dealer can supply, you will be able to select a camera whose type, features, and capabilities are accurately attuned to your needs.

39

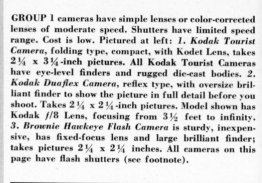

CAMERA TYPES AND FEATURES

GROUP 1 cameras have simple lenses or color-corrected lenses of moderate speed. Shutters have limited speed range. Cost is low. Pictured at left: *1. Kodak Tourist Camera*, folding type, compact, with Kodet Lens, takes 2¼ x 3¼-inch pictures. All Kodak Tourist Cameras have eye-level finders and rugged die-cast bodies. *2. Kodak Duaflex Camera*, reflex type, with oversize brilliant finder to show the picture in full detail before you shoot. Takes 2¼ x 2¼-inch pictures. Model shown has Kodak *f*/8 Lens, focusing from 3½ feet to infinity. *3. Brownie Hawkeye Flash Camera* is sturdy, inexpensive, has fixed-focus lens and large brilliant finder; takes pictures 2¼ x 2¼ inches. All cameras on this page have flash shutters (see footnote).

GROUP 2 cameras have faster lenses (*f*/6.3 and *f*/4.5), fully color-corrected; faster shutters, focusing adjustment, and other picture-taking refinements. Pictured at left: *4. Kodak Tourist Camera f/4.5* has Kodak Anaston *f*/4.5 Lens in Flash Kodamatic 1/200 Shutter. Another *f*/4.5 model has a super-speed Kodak Synchro-Rapid Shutter, 1/800 second. Picture size is 2¼ x 3¼ inches; an accessory kit permits three other sizes. *5. Kodak Flash Bantam f/4.5 Camera* is a true "miniature"— weighs 13 ounces, is 4⅝ inches long. 6 and 7, *Kodak Pony 828* and *Pony 135 Cameras* are smart, low-cost miniature cameras with *f*/4.5 lenses and shutter speeds to 1/200 second.

GROUP 3 cameras have very fast lenses (*f*/3.5 or even faster) and operating refinements rarely found in Group 1 or 2 cameras. Pictured at left: *8. Kodak Reflex II Camera* is focusing-type twin-lens reflex; has twin Kodak Anastar *f*/3.5 Lenses, flash-synchronizing 1/300-second shutter, ground-glass viewing screen backed by an Ektalite Field Lens which doubles the image brilliance. Takes 2¼ x 2¼-inch pictures, 12 to each roll of film. *9. Kodak Medalist II Camera* combines larger picture size (2¼ x 3¼ inches) with the precision and operating refinements of a fine miniature camera. It has a Kodak Ektar *f*/3.5 Lens; Kodak Flash Supermatic 1/400 Shutter; lens-coupled range finder focusing, with automatic parallax correction for view finder; film advance with automatic shutter cocking; exposure counter; double-exposure prevention. In performance, quality, and versatility, it's unequaled.

◀ The flash-synchronized shutter has become an essential identifying feature of a truly modern camera— both beginners' types and advanced types. Every Kodak Camera pictured on this page has flash contacts built into the shutter, and accepts an inexpensive accessory Kodak Flasholder (one type is shown here on the Brownie Hawkeye Flash Camera).

40

PICTURE-TAKING SCOPE (the reflex cameras take square pictures)

GROUP 1 cameras are entirely adequate for snapshots, in good daylight, of non-moving or slow-moving subjects, and for flood and flash snapshots. Beginners like their simplicity of operation. Such cameras yield excellent record shots of buildings, scenic views, family activities where there is no fast motion, pets, and other everyday subjects which make up the bulk of a family picture collection. Naturally, these cameras cannot offer you the broad picture scope of a fine fast-lens camera.

GROUP 2 cameras embrace all the subjects indicated above, plus subjects in fairly rapid motion, subjects in shady spots, outdoor activities on dull or overcast days, back-lighted subjects where full shadow detail is required, and indoor photoflood or photoflash shots at greater lamp-to-subject distances. Their greater lens speed and shutter speed permit dozens of pictures that would be impossible for anyone to obtain with a simple-lens camera.

GROUP 3 cameras embrace all the subjects in Groups 1 and 2 — plus fast-action subjects, moving subjects under difficult light conditions, indoor snapshots or very short "time" exposures without special photo lights, snaps at night sports events and on well-lighted theater stages, shots of brightly-lighted street scenes at night, full-color snapshots of illuminated signs, fast-action snaps in full color on bright days, full-color flood or flash shots at greater lamp-to-subject ranges or with fewer lamps—a great range of fascinating material that is beyond the capacity of slower lenses and slower shutters. In addition, the picture-taking refinements of the Group 3 cameras— such as range-finder focusing or ground-glass focusing, double-exposure prevention, and so on — make picture taking easier, quicker, and more fun. These are the cameras the real picture-taking enthusiasts use.

41

A BIT LATER, we'll review cameras in detail. But first, let's examine the essentials of a fine camera.

the lens, diaphragm, and shutter

Quite a few of the important devices on a camera are light-control devices. The lens is a very important feature; it determines what pictures you can take, under what light conditions, and how sharply detailed they will be.

The lens collects rays of light from each point of your subject, and focuses them back to a corresponding point on the film. The larger the lens opening, *compared to its distance from the film,* the greater its relative light-collecting power:

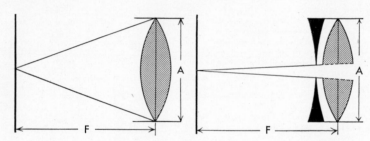

This is a cross section of a very fast lens. Note ratio of aperture A to focal length F.

This is a low-speed lens (or a high-speed lens closed down to a small aperture).

what the "f" numbers mean

Those curious numbers you see on a fine lens, such as $f/2$ or $f/4$, indicate the relative "speed" of the lens. Actually, $f/2$ is a short way to say "focal length is twice the diameter of the lens opening," and the diagram at left shows exactly what that means. This might be a lens one-half inch across, which takes sharp pictures of faraway objects when the midpoint of the lens is exactly one

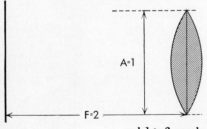

... and 1-to-2 equals $f/2$

inch from the film. It could also be a lens with an opening three inches across, which forms an image at six inches, and the ratio would still be one-to-two, or $f/2$. This "f-system" makes it possible to compare the speed of any lenses, large or small, and to provide exposure recommendations which will be correct for both small and large cameras.

"slow" and "fast" lenses

An $f/2$, $f/3.5$, or $f/4.5$ lens is usually called a "fast" lens. An $f/16$ or $f/11$ lens is called a "slow" lens; and if you remember that a lens collects light with its entire surface, you'll see why. This diagram shows the difference, and explains why an $f/2$ lens is *sixty-four* times as fast as an $f/16$ lens:

f/2   f/4   f/5.6   f/8   f/16

$f/2$ is 64 times as large as $f/16$ on the same lens, and passes 64 times as much light as $f/16$. On a big studio camera lens, the $f/16$ opening may be larger than $f/2$ on a miniature camera lens — but the $f/2$ is still 64 times as "fast" as $f/16$.

Compute it this way:

$f/2 \times f/2$ is 1/4
$f/16 \times f/16$ is 1/256
$256 \div 4$ is **64**

Speed, however, is not the whole story of a fine lens. A slow lens can be made of one piece of glass. But a Kodak Ektar, Anaston, or Anastar Lens must be built up of several pieces or "elements" of special glass, very accurately formed, polished, and mounted together with great precision. This not only permits the construction of very high-power lenses, but also permits the correction of optical errors which cannot be corrected in a single-element lens. Therefore, the fine lens can take *sharper* pictures than can the simple Brownie lens, whether it is used at its largest opening or is "stopped down" to a small opening such as $f/8$, $f/11$, $f/16$, or $f/22$.

43

Study the cut-away cross section of a fine Kodak lens—and you begin to appreciate the optical and mechanical skill it requires. Each element must be of perfect glass, ground to exact curvature, and fitted into a mount of extreme precision.

the iris diaphragm—your camera's front gate

In bright light, you do not always need all the speed of a fine lens; and so, an *iris diaphragm* is provided in such lenses. This can be opened up or closed down, to admit just the right amount of light to the film.

Your eye also has an iris, which closes down automatically in bright light, and opens wide in dim light. The difference in the camera iris is that you make the adjustment by hand. ⬇

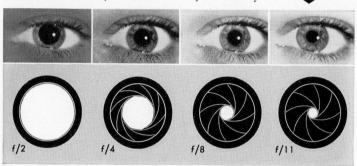

f/2   f/4   f/8   f/11

your camera shutter—the inner gate

The iris diaphragm gate stands ajar all the time, but your camera's second gate—its shutter—opens only when you take a picture.

The shutter of an inexpensive camera may be a simple metal plate, actuated by a spring. The shutter fitted to a fine fast lens is quite different. Such shutters as the precisely-made Kodak Supermatic have several blades of fine steel, operated by a series of gears of the type you find in a good watch. Indeed, the whole shutter is constructed with the care that goes into watchmaking. Instead of offering just one snapshot speed, it may provide eight or nine speeds—ranging, say, from one full second up to 1/800.

44

Practically all fine shutters (and many simple ones) now also have built-in flash synchronizing mechanism, to fire a photoflash lamp during the period the shutter is open.

Here's a glimpse inside a fine Kodak shutter. As you can see, it resembles the interior of a fine watch—and as a matter of fact it is made with watchlike precision.

the focusing movement

Your eye focuses automatically when you look at near objects, and changes focus when you shift to faraway objects. A camera with a fast lens has a special "focusing" adjustment to take care of this, with a distance scale marked in feet.

At any setting of the focusing movement, a lens covers sharply a certain zone. For example, a lens set at "15 feet" may picture sharply everything beyond 10 feet up to 25 feet from the camera. Close it down to a smaller opening, and the zone widens both toward and away from you. Open the lens wide, and the zone of sharp focus or "depth of field" is reduced.

The nearer your camera is to your subject, the smaller the depth of field. Also, the larger the lens opening you use, the smaller the depth of field. Therefore, when you are using a large lens opening, or when you are taking close-up shots, you always measure the distance from lens to subject with particular care.

For measuring distances, some cameras have built-in range finders, which are connected or "coupled" to the focusing movement. As the lens is focused, two images in the range finder move into line with each other. When they are aligned, the camera lens is in correct focus for the object imaged in the range finder. 45

These dominoes show how the "depth of field" changes as you change the lens opening. At left, the camera was focused on the ball, and a large lens opening used. The nearest and farthest dominoes are "out of focus"— quite blurred. Sometimes, by using a large lens opening, you can completely "focus out" an undesirable background.

At right, the camera is still focused on the ball —but now we use a small lens opening. All the dominoes, near and far, are sharp. On Page 77 you will find a handy "depth" table, with the proper settings for any subject.

Professional view cameras have ground-glass focusing backs, which permit the user to focus a scene full picture size on a ground-glass screen. The more elaborate fast-lensed twin-lens reflex cameras also use this principle (see cutaway at left); the upper lens is a "viewing lens" with a mirror behind it and a ground glass above it. Many advanced workers feel a ground glass has unique advantages; but, of course, the ground-glass image cannot be expected to match the detail and clarity of the big "brilliant" finders used on the simple twin-lens reflexes (see below).

advantages of specific camera types

Although used by few experts, the simple box-type camera has two outstanding advantages: low cost, and simplicity of operation. For a beginner's camera, it is surpassed only by the simple reflex-type cameras, such as the Kodak Duaflex and Brownie Reflex Cameras. These moderately-priced reflex cameras have the great advantage of a super-sized brilliant finder, which shows details of the subject with crystal clarity and in relatively large scale. Such a view finder is of tremendous aid to the beginner; it gives him a much clearer idea of what his picture will include, and assists him in framing and composition (just as the ground-glass focusing panel of an advanced reflex camera assists the expert). In all other features, the simple reflex cameras are as easy to operate as the box camera.

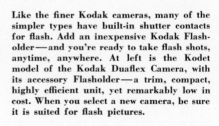

Like the finer Kodak cameras, many of the simpler types have built-in shutter contacts for flash. Add an inexpensive Kodak Flasholder — and you're ready to take flash shots, anytime, anywhere. At left is the Kodet model of the Kodak Duaflex Camera, with its accessory Flasholder — a trim, compact, highly efficient unit, yet remarkably low in cost. When you select a new camera, be sure it is suited for flash pictures.

advantages of the folding camera

Folding cameras, such as the Kodak Tourist Cameras, excel all other types in relative compactness — that is, picture size compared to camera size. They offer a wide range of choices, from simple beginners' types to models for the expert. Because of their compact form and ease of transportation, they are perennial favorites for all-around family use.

There are four efficient, smartly styled models of the Kodak Tourist Camera. This is the popular f/4.5 standard model — shown with accessory Kodak Flasholder.

versatility of the Kodak "Tourists"

One of the first questions about any camera is, "How many things will it do?" All four of the Kodak Tourist Cameras have flash shutters; add a simple Kodak Flasholder, and they perform indoors, or after dark, as capably as in the daytime. The two f/4.5 models and the f/6.3 model have ample lens speed for snapshots on dull days, and for action shots. The f/4.5 "800" model has a top shutter speed of 1/800 second — an extraordinary speed, adequate for extremely fast sports action. And by adding an inexpensive Kodak Tourist Adapter Kit (at right) to any of these three cameras, you have a choice of four picture sizes—the regular 2¼x3¼-inch pictures, plus 2¼x2¼, 1⅝x2¼, and No. 828 — on black-and-white film, or Kodacolor, or No. 828 Kodachrome Film!

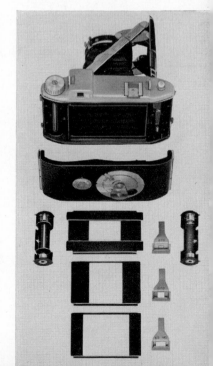

47

advantages of the Kodak Medalist II Camera

Unique among cameras, the Kodak Medalist II Camera is built with the precision of a fine miniature camera and has all the refinements of such cameras (including coupled range finder), yet it takes 2¼x3¼-inch pictures either on roll film or, with an accessory back, on film pack and sheet film. Thus, it is adaptable to all the specialized films available to professional photographers, as well as the popular amateur films. With the accessory back, ground-glass focusing can be used, and back extension units are available for extreme close-up work on small subjects and specimens. The camera's *f*/3.5 Kodak Ektar Lens, of course, offers an exceptional degree of sharpness and color correction; and its Kodak Supermatic Shutter, with speeds up to 1/400 second, equips it for fast-action subjects. For the expert amateur, scientist, news photographer, and photographic illustrator, it offers a combination of qualities found in no other camera.

At left, the unique, highly versatile Kodak Medalist II Camera — a camera that combines miniature-camera precision with big-camera performance. Not only is the Medalist's *f*/3.5 Kodak Ektar Lens the finest ever installed on a 2¼x3¼ camera — but also every other detail of this superb camera is designed to assure top optical and mechanical performance. The big, rigid, all-metal double-helix focusing mount — the ultra-precise coupled range finder — and every other feature — are planned for the finest possible performance.

For real economy in a capable miniature camera, pick the Kodak Pony 135 Camera (at right) or the Kodak Pony 828 Camera. Each has a crisply corrected Kodak Anaston *f*/4.5 Lens, flash-synchronizing shutter with speeds to 1/200, and ultra-smooth shutter release; basic exposure settings for black-and-white and color are indexed in red, making these cameras as easy to operate as a box camera!

advantages of the miniature camera

Small size, high precision, fast lenses and fast shutters, and adaptability to Kodachrome Film for full-color transparencies — these are the virtues of fine miniature cameras such as the Kodak Pony 135 and 828 Cameras, and the Kodak Flash Bantam $f/4.5$ Camera. Don't judge these cameras on picture size. Although the negatives are small, the precision of the lenses is such that fine enlargements can be made to full exhibition size; and for album use, standard enlarged prints, 2¾x4 inches, can be had from modern photofinishers.

now, what about the film?

There's a Kodak film for every need. Those most used by amateur photographers are:

Kodak Verichrome Film — This is a fast *orthochromatic* film, for daylight shots and photoflash shots. *"Orthochromatic"* means the film is sensitive to all visible light except red; therefore, this film can be developed under a red safelight in the darkroom. More Kodak Verichrome Film is used for amateur snapshots than any other film.

Kodak Super-XX Film — This is a very high-speed *panchromatic* film, for indoor shots with photoflood lamps, flash shots when high-speed film is required, and outdoor snapshots under difficult light conditions. *"Panchromatic"* means that the film is sensitive to *all* visible light, *including* red; therefore, panchromatic film must be developed in complete darkness, with only occasional help from a dim green safelight.

Kodak Plus-X Film — This is a fine-grain panchromatic film. Because of the fine texture of the silver image, it is especially suited for pictures from which enlargements are to be made.

Kodak Panatomic-X Film — This is an ultra-fine-grain panchromatic film, for miniature cameras only. It is the favorite miniature camera film for large-scale enlargements from very small negatives.

All these are films for black-and-white pictures. The Kodak films for full-color pictures are reviewed in Chapter 7, Page 53.

accessories for picture taking

Good film and a good camera — these are basic equipment for all first-class photography. As you progress, you'll want to add certain accessories which broaden the scope of your picture taking.

First accessory, by far, is a flash synchronizer (or an inexpensive Kodak Flasholder, if you have a Kodak camera with a flash-synchronizing shutter). This equipment extends your camera's day right around the clock — lets you take pictures anywhere, day or night, by means of photoflash lamps. Outdoors, in the daytime, it enables you to take better shots "against the light" or in dense shade — as any expert news or magazine photographer will tell you.

"reading glasses" for your camera

Next — a Kodak Close-Up Attachment, or one or more Kodak Portra Lenses. These permit you to take true close-ups (see below). They simply slip on over the camera lens, and require no change in exposure. The Close-Up Attachment is ideal for close-up shots of pets and small children, and informal portraits of adults, especially with fixed-focus cameras. Portra Lenses are ideal for close-ups of flowers, table-top shots, and many other small subjects.

filters, for pictorial work

Next — one or more color filters for use with black-and-white film. These are devices to subdue certain colors of light, while allowing other colors to pass through the lens. For example, a Kodak Wratten K-2 Filter absorbs blue light, but passes other colors. In an outdoor shot the K-2 subdues part of the blue light

At left, picture taken without Kodak Portra Lens; next, with the Kodak Portra 1+ . . . Kodak Portra 2+ . . . and Kodak Portra 3+

| Panchromatic film, no filter | "Pan" film; yellow (K2) filter | "Pan" film; red (A) filter |

from the sky; therefore (see above) the sky has richer tone in your pictures, and clouds stand out better. You might start with a K-2 Filter, and later add a Kodak Wratten A Filter, which yields dramatic dark-sky effects on panchromatic film.

Since a filter cuts off some light, it requires a certain increase in exposure. This increase is stated as a multiplying "factor" for each film. Suppose you are using a K-2 Filter with Kodak Plus-X Film; the factor is 2. If a subject calls for 1/50 second at $f/11$ without the filter, then the correct exposure *with* the filter is 1/50 at $f/8$ (since $f/8$ is twice as large a lens opening as $f/11$). It's as simple as that. Whenever $f/11$ is correct without a filter, and you want to use a filter at the same shutter speed—

If the factor is: 2	2.5*	3*	4	5*	6*	8	10*	12	16
Set the lens at: $f/8$		$f/5.6$			$f/4$		$f/3.5$	$f/2.8$	

*For these factors, set the pointer between the two indicated f/numbers.

camera supports—and cases

For exposures longer than 1/50 second, a solid camera support is desirable — either a simple pocket support such as the Koda-pod or Kodak Optipod, or a compact, lightweight tripod. The Kodak Eye-Level Tripod is the best choice, but there are other sturdy Kodak tripods at economical prices.

And, last but not least—a carrying case to protect your camera. A fine camera deserves such protection. It's so important that fine leather carrying cases are included with certain of the top-level Kodak cameras.

Correct exposure produces the best pictures, and it's merely a matter of using the right lens opening and shutter speed—to fit the film, light conditions, type of subject, and any *motion* in the subject. This table is for black-and-white films. The "action" column A shows the shutter speeds for moving and non-moving subjects. Other columns show the lens openings ("*f*" numbers); **S** is for brilliant sunny days, **H** for HAZY sun; **C** for CLOUDY-bright days. *Example:* On a sunny day, with Kodak Verichrome Film, to picture a group playing badminton on a beach, set the shutter at 1/400 and the lens at *f*/5.6. If your shutter is not that fast, risk 1/300 at *f*/6.3 or 1/200 at *f*/8.

52

TYPE OF SUBJECT		SUBJECT MOTION	A	The Kodak Film You're Using								
				Verichrome or Plus-X			Super-XX			Panatomic-X		
		⬇		S	H	C	S	H	C	S	H	C
	Broad, open beach or snow scenes, with no prominent dark objects in foreground	Little	1/100	16	11	8	22	16	11	11	8	5.6
		None	1/50	22	16	11	32	22	16	16	11	8
	Nearby people on beaches, in snow, or other highly reflective surroundings	Fast	1/400	5.6	4	2.8	8	5.6	4	4	2.8	2
		Fast	1/300	6.3	4.5	3.5	9	6.3	4.5	4.5	3.5	2.5
		Slow	1/200	8	5.6	4	11	8	5.6	5.6	4	2.8
		Slow	1/100	11	8	5.6	16	11	8	8	5.6	4
		None	1/50	16	11	8	22	16	11	11	8	5.6
	Nearby people in average scenes (lawns, fields, gardens) NOT IN SHADE	Fast	1/400	4	2.8	2	5.6	4	2.8	2.8	2	
		Fast	1/300	4.5	3.5	2.5	6.3	4.5	3.5	3.5	2.5	2
		Slow	1/200	5.6	4	2.8	8	5.6	4	4	2.8	2
		Slow	1/100	8	5.6	4	11	8	5.6	5.6	4	2.8
		None	1/50	11	8	6.3	16	11	8	8	5.6	4
	People and nearby scenes backlighted or in "open shade" (facing open sky) NOT UNDER TREES OR PORCHES	Fast	1/400	2.8	2		4	2.8	2	2		
		Slow	1/100	5.6	4	2.8	8	5.6	4	4	2.8	2
		None	1/50	8	5.6	4	11	8	5.6	5.6	4	2.8
		None	1/25	11	8	5.6	16	11	8	8	5.6	4

A basic setting for outdoor shots of average subjects on sunny days with Kodak Verichrome Film is 1/50 at *f*/11, camera focused at 15 feet.

← More convenient than exposure tables are the **Snapshot Kodaguide** and **Flash Kodaguide** — inexpensive pocket-size exposure computers, easy to carry, easy to use. Let your Kodak dealer show you how they work.

Pictures
in full color

LOAD A KODAK FULL-COLOR FILM into your camera, and you're equipped to shoot pictures in full color.

Now—without special equipment—without elaborate training —you can capture the rainbow and bring it home.

Which camera? Practically every camera made today will accept full-color film. And most of the older cameras, too. Kodak makes full-color films that are fast enough to be used in Brownie cameras; others are especially suited to use in miniature cameras; still others for sheet-film cameras. Some yield prints on paper; others produce sparkling full-color transparencies for screen projection or direct viewing, and from these transparencies full-color prints can also be made.

Never before have amateur photographers had this colorful world so completely at their command.

the Kodak full-color films

For amateur roll-film cameras, Kodacolor Film is the proper film. You load it and expose it just as any other film. Your dealer sends it to the Eastman Kodak Company, which processes it, obtaining full-color *negatives* in which all the colors are complementary to those of your subject. Then positive prints are made —as many as your order calls for, from each negative.

Later on, at any time, you can order through your Kodak dealer any number of additional prints from any negative. Often a color enthusiast will order several dozen prints of a favorite shot, for use as Christmas greetings or anniversary announcements. This practice is growing every year.

All Kodacolor Prints are made about 3½ inches in the narrow dimension — which usually means that the print is larger than the original negative. For example, a 2¼x3¼-inch negative yields a print about 3½x5 inches, while 2¼x2¼ or 1⅝x1⅝ negatives yield prints about 3½ inches square. In addition, Kodacolor *Enlargements* can be ordered, 5x7, 8x10, or 11x14 inches.

Regular Kodacolor Film is for daylight use. Type A Kodacolor Film is for use with photoflood and photoflash lamps.

Like other color films and prints discussed here, Kodacolor Film, Kodacolor Prints, and Kodacolor Enlargements contain dyes. These are as stable as possible consistent with their other requirements; but prolonged exposure to bright daylight, and especially to bright sunlight, should be avoided. Since all dyes may, in time, fade, the Eastman Kodak Company does not warrant any color films, negatives, transparencies, or prints against change in color.

The price of a roll of Kodacolor Film includes development of the film, but not the cost of prints.

Kodachrome Film—several types

Kodachrome Film is quite different from Kodacolor Film. Instead of a negative, it produces a full-color positive transparency. This can be viewed on an illuminator such as the Kodaslide Table Viewer, or projected in large size on a wall screen.

There are several types of Kodachrome Film—in sizes for various cameras. For Miniature cameras (Kodak Bantam or 35mm. cameras), there's Kodachrome Film, Daylight Type (to be used in daylight) and Type A (for use with photoflood lamps). By using the correct filters over the camera lens, the daylight type can be adapted for photoflood use, or the Type A adapted for daylight use. In addition, for sheet-film cameras, there are Kodachrome Professional Film, Daylight Type (for daylight) and Type B (for use with professional studio lamps).

After exposure, Kodachrome Film is mailed to the nearest

Eastman Kodak Company processing station which handles that particular form of Kodachrome Film. Cost of processing is included in the price of the film, and it is returned to you ready for viewing or projection.

If you want additional transparencies you can order duplicates through your Kodak dealer; and you can also order enlarged Kodachrome Prints—in a variety of sizes, from about the size of a playing card up to 8x11 inches or larger.

points to watch in color shooting

It's easy to "shoot it in color"—if you heed a few elementary points of technique.

First — *use the right film for the light.*

For outdoor daylight shots, use Kodachrome Film, Daylight Type, or Kodacolor Film.

For indoor daylight shots, when your camera is loaded with a daylight film, leave the window shades up, and use a *blue-bulb* photoflash lamp if extra light is needed. If your camera is loaded with Kodachrome (or Kodacolor) Film, Type A, pull down the shades and use *only* photoflood or photoflash light.

For pictures after dark, use regular flood or flash lamps with Type A Kodacolor or Kodachrome Film; or *blue-bulb* flash lamps if your camera is loaded with a daylight film. A filter is needed with most flash lamps; you'll find complete recommendations for filters, and exposure data for both Kodachrome and Kodacolor Film, Type A, on Page 160.

Second point of technique — *correct location and lighting of your subject, for best color rendering.*

A soft lighting, without intense contrasts of light and shade, is best for color pictures. When picturing people indoors, arrange your photo lamps to eliminate harsh shadows. Outdoors, select a camera position and subject placement that minimizes such shadows. The best color quality is obtained outdoors in bright or hazy sunlight. A reflector of white paper, a white sheet, or even a white house wall, can be used to soften undesirable shadows on a subject's face. If your camera is photoflash-synchronized, a *blue-bulb* flash lamp can often be used to soften the shadows in sunny-day shots taken at moderate distances.

Third point — *correct exposure.*

Color films demand more exact exposure than do black-and-white films. Err in exposure, and the color goes "off"— it turns pale and weak with overexposure, or dark and muddy with underexposure. With every roll of Kodak color film, you will find a reliable exposure table, covering all average conditions; follow its advice, and you'll be on safe ground. Even more convenient is a Snapshot Kodaguide or Flash Kodaguide. And for unusual or "problem" conditions, a photoelectric exposure meter, if correctly used, can be a real help. But whatever exposure aid you use, take care to follow its indications to the letter.

other points for fine work

There are some other points to watch after you have made your first color shots. They don't matter so much in casual snaps —
but you'll soon want to progress to more artistic work, such as

Kodachrome Film, and how it's viewed

Kodachrome Film for miniature cameras yields full-color transparencies, which come back to you mounted as 2x2-inch slides, like this. You can view these slides directly, or show them in a Kodaslide Table Viewer, at left, which gives a brilliant, magnified image even in a fully lighted room. Or, you can project them in large size on a home screen.

With a Kodaslide Projector, Master Model, ➡ you can project Kodachrome slides to fill a theater or auditorium screen.

Home projectors such as the popular Kodaslide Projector Model 2A, below, or the inexpensive 1A, at left below, enable you to show your Kodachrome slides in impressive size — several feet wide on the screen — much as movies are projected. It's fun to put on a full-color show for friends and guests. You can also have enlarged prints made in full color, for gifts or home decoration.

KODACHROME

KODACHROME

informal portraits in color, flower close-ups, table-top scenes, and still-life studies.

The most important of these points are color harmony, color arrangement, and *contrast* — both color contrast and contrast of light and shade.

In nature, most of the color combinations tend to be pleasing and harmonious — not clashing, garish, noisy. You will do well, when you select or arrange your subjects, to follow that example. Most beginners crowd too much raw color into their pictures — violent reds, greens, purples, yellows. That's not only unnecessary, but dead wrong. A very small amount of color will produce

tips for pleasant color pictures

Use the right film. In daylight, Kodachrome or Kodacolor Film, Daylight Type. For flood or flash shots, Kodachrome or Kodacolor Film, Type A.

Expose accurately. A Snapshot Kodaguide, at left, quickly gives you the right lens opening and shutter speed. For unusual conditions, a photoelectric exposure meter is useful.

Avoid contrasty lighting. For most shots, have the light behind you and full on the subject, as above. Color contrast is usually enough, without light-and-shadow contrast.

Don't "cheat" on exposure. When the Kodaguide indicates a lens opening halfway between two marked openings, it means just that — no more, no less.

For steadiness, when your shutter speed is less than 1/50 second, use a camera support. A Kodapod, left, is very handy.

a pleasing picture; consider, for example, a snow scene with a few dark evergreens and delicate blue shadows on the snow. Subtle, yet complete. Big splashes of "poster color" are exciting at first, but discriminating photographers soon outgrow them and turn toward gentler harmonies.

Color arrangement follows, in some measure, the rules of black-and-white pictorial composition. The picture, as a whole, should appear pleasantly balanced and well-organized—not too "heavy" on one side, nor scattered. Your eye should be led in, and should go naturally to a center of interest, and rest there. To this end, remember that vivid reds and yellows tend to excite   59

(Continued on Page 65)

Hazy sunshine is ideal for close-up pictures of people — shadows are soft and full of detail.

Light reflectors, such as the white house wall above, help in sidelighted shots.

Kodak Portra Lenses allow close views of small subjects, such as flowers, blossoms, nature subjects, pets.

Bright beaches, snow, and other light-reflecting surroundings offer helpful shadow illumination.

BASIC EXPOSURES in bright sun, with average subjects, front-lighted (facing the light), are: Kodachrome Film, Daylight Type, 1/50 second at $f/6.3$ (halfway between $f/5.6$ and $f/8$); Kodacolor Film, Daylight Type, 1/50 second at $f/11$. For other lighting conditions and for photoflood and photoflash exposures, see the Kodaguides.

Color subjects may be rich
and vivid, as in these Kodacolor
Prints of autumn and winter scenes. Or, the color
may be subtle and delicate, as in the waterfall scene (next page) ...

...which is reproduced from a full-color transparency on Kodachrome Film. No matter what the season, you'll find color opportunities wherever you go.

more tips for pleasing color pictures

A large window and a reflector (a white sheet or large white card) provide a handy setup for indoor daylight pictures of people. Use a daylight type film, of course.

↑
Keep the main lights near the camera axis (line from camera to subject). Be sure light is on subject.

↑
A separate light may be used to brighten the background and subdue any shadows cast by the subject.

For color shots, balance your lights so there are no deep, harsh shadows. In this picture, two lights were used—one at the left, back of the subject, and one at the right of the stove. If a single light is used, keep it as close to the camera as possible. Color contrast takes the place of light-and-shade in a color shot; in this one, if it were color, the brown turkey, hair, and flesh tones would stand out very sharply against the wall, which is probably pale green, blue, ⇐ or cream-colored.

Watch out for noisy patterns! In black-and-white, this floral print gives no trouble, because the colors record as gray—but in color the smock would steal the picture. For an example in full color, look on Page 64, upper left picture. (If you can't eliminate such a pattern, try putting it in shadow; that often helps.) ➡

Snow shadows under a blue sky are blue
—almost the same color as the sky. Color
film captures this, even through your eye
fails to see it. For a full-color example of
blue snow shadows, see Page 109. ➡

Think in color — see in color. The far
plane will pick up some color from the
sky, and (in the shadowed areas) some
color from the land. The foreground
plane will retain its own color, subdued
by shadow, if it's parked on a neutral
gray concrete runway. On grass, it will
be its own color, plus a touch of green,
plus shadow. ⬇

Seek simple backgrounds, just as in black-and-
white shots. Black and gray backgrounds are
neutral. Cool colors (such as green and cold
blue) make desirable backgrounds; they tend
to recede from your eye, while warm colors
tend to "come toward you." Note the soft
lighting and open shadows in the flower. ➡

Any good sunset is better in color; 1/25 second
at f/6.3 is about average exposure for a sunset on Kodachrome Film. Underexposure gives
deeper, richer colors; overexposure lightens
them into pastel tints. ⬇

colorful vs. good color

To use a great deal of brilliant color in a color picture is a natural temptation.

For example, the picture at the left, above, is a veritable "color hash." It's colorful, unquestionably—so colorful that the model is practically lost in a blaze of assorted hues. At the right, above, a better picture is achieved in terms of less obtrusive colors and a simple sky background.

At the left, below, is shown the unfortunate result of permitting the model's face to be colored by light passing through or reflected from an accessory. The green parasol is the villain in this case. In the picture at the right, the parasol has been left out; the model's face appears as it should.

In other words, simplicity and harmony are even greater virtues in color photography than in black-and-white.

your eye and draw attention; therefore, they are helpful as accents at or near the center of interest. Cool dark colors, on the other hand, tend to recede — so that gray-greens, blue-greens, dark blues, and deep browns are especially useful as backgrounds. Such colors are also helpful at the edges and corners of a picture; they tend to hold the composition together. A small, vividly colored accent in a composition has an effective "weight" or "attention value" out of all proportion to its size; it will balance or outweigh a much larger area of dark or subdued color.

For most color shots, the various colors provide enough contrast, and contrast of *light and shade* should be kept low. This is especially true if important details lie in the shadow portions of your subject, or if correct color rendering is desired in the shadows. A shadow will seem reasonably light to your eye, because the iris of the eye adjusts automatically; but it is still quite dark to the film. Therefore, when you want full detail and accurate color in the shadow areas, you should adjust the lighting (by means of reflectors in daylight shots, and placement of the lights in artificially lighted shots) until shadows are barely visible.

Sometimes, however, you will want a more vigorous effect, in order to present a subject in a more dramatic manner, or obtain some special interpretive effect. In that event, do not hesitate to employ strong lighting contrast. Base your exposure on the brilliantly lighted parts of the picture, and let the *shadows* go black. You lose in shadow detail, but you often gain a dividend in pictorial strength.

making use of your color shots

Pictures are made to be seen and used — and this applies to color shots as fully as to black-and-whites. Color prints brighten up the album; color enlargements make superb wall decorations and gifts; color transparencies, when properly organized for projection, provide entertainment for the family and for guests. For the collector, the educator, and many others, color provides unique advantages. You'll find more details on these points when you reach Chapter 21, Page 197.

Part II

Getting down to cases

You NOW KNOW practically everything that's basic to good picture taking. From now on, your success will depend mostly on your own discernment — your judgment in selecting subject matter, and in handling subject matter after you've selected it.

The chapters that follow will help you on those points. They'll suggest places, subjects, and picture ideas. Tucked in, here and there, where they seem most useful, you'll also find additional hints on picture-taking technique. Many of these hints have a wide application. For instance, in the chapter on flower pictures, you'll learn why a panchromatic film is better than an orthochromatic film when you're taking pictures of a red rose. The same rule also applies when you're picturing a red barn, or a person in a red dress. In the chapter on "Picturing People," you'll find suggestions about how to place your lights in order to bring out the shape of a subject's face and features. The same techniques apply to other subjects when you want them to stand out with an effect of roundness and solid form.

Always remember one thing. It's as easy to take a good picture as a poor one, and a lot more satisfying. Within a few months, if you apply what you've learned, your album should be bulging with as many good pictures as this book contains. And that, by the way, offers an interesting comparison in values. This book costs you little. Your album, properly filled with your own pictures, is an almost priceless possession.

66

Pictures
right around home

WHY ROAM FAR AFIELD in search of picture material — when the best hunting-ground of all is at home, right under your nose?

Every day, every hour, there's a new fund of picture possibilities. Such occasions as Christmas, Thanksgiving, birthdays — these are crests on the tide of events, and we'll examine them in detail later on. But in between —

How many snapshots do you have of Johnny, biting into that big after-school slab of bread and jam?

Did you keep a shot of that gorgeous big bunch of jonquils when they burst into bloom early last spring, in the bowl on your sunny kitchen-window sill?

Where's the moonlight shot of the snow-covered lawn, through the living-room window?

Where's the shot of the roaring blaze in the fireplace, with the

Tough times in the old tub. Tears make pictures too.➡

Keep your camera handy, to catch the everyday scenes that mean so much. ⬇

Remember to watch ➡ the lighting and background. In this charming shot, the dark porch offers an ideal background for the sunlit child.

room lights dimmed, and the children toasting marshmallows?

Where's the shot of Dad, sound asleep by the lawn mower, after ten minutes' work in early summer?

Where's the series of shots that were taken — well, that *should* have been taken — when you put the garden in?

Where's the series of shots showing the carving of the big jack-o'-lantern — to supplement the shot of the lighted lantern in the window?

Where are the color shots of the trees in their flaming autumn dress, and the color shots of the leaf-raking and the bonfires?

You didn't take them? Well, never mind. *Some* of the opportunities will come again. They won't be quite the same. Each member of the family will be a little older. There will be gaps in the family story that can't be patched up now. But you *can* begin, today, to write the rest of the story as it should be written — clear, comprehensive, and complete.

few things are "too unimportant" for pictures

Most of us suffer from an unfortunate mental quirk. We think that something must be new, unusual, extraordinary — or it doesn't deserve a picture. Starting on a vacation tour, our first thought is for a camera, and a plentiful supply of film. But at home, the camera often remains tucked away, *empty* — while a hundred picture opportunities come and go, each as worthwhile as any vacation picture.

It's the small things—the daily, intimate events—that yield the best pictures. Overlook them, and you're wasting pure gold. Capture them, no matter how trivial they may seem at the moment — and you'll treasure them forever.

Load up your camera, now, and we'll take a tour around a reasonably typical household, spotting opportunities and making practical suggestions as we go.

first, we'll poke around the yard a bit—

Let's say it's a sunny day in late spring. We come up to the front

68

Activity makes the picture. Let your subjects be doing something—not just standing still for the camera. And don't feel that a front view is always essential. These back views prove it isn't.

gate, and find Jenny is using it for a swing. Small girls know what gates are for — and wise parents know that an album isn't complete without pictures of that operation.

(Eight or ten years from now, in another springtime, Jenny will be leaning on that same gate, swapping sweet words with the boy from next door. She won't want anybody to take a picture of that, naturally; but she'll be using her own camera to picture this boy, and other boys in her high school class.)

Wind the film, and keep your eye open for other activities. It's *activity* — not necessarily fast motion, but merely "something going on"— that makes pictures interesting.

As we pass through the gate, you make a note of the budding roses. They're not quite ready yet — but in a few weeks, they'll be offering other pictures for you to take.

snaps are busting out all over!

Grandfather is busily snipping away at the hedge. That should be good for a close-up. You focus (or slip a Kodak Close-Up Attachment over the lens of your nonfocusing camera). His broad hat brim shades his face, but his white shirt and shirtsleeve reflect light up into the shadows, making them "open" and bright. So you use a normal "bright sunshine" exposure — 1/50 second at *f*/11, on Kodak Verichrome or Kodak Plus-X Film — or a regular snapshot exposure if yours is a simpler type of camera.

by the way—where's Dad?

Your picture-roving eye rests on the hammock — and, sure enough, there's the head of the house, gallantly throwing himself into the spring cleanup. His arm hangs down toward the magazine he's dropped; and a look of perfect bliss wreathes his sleeping face.

It's shady under the freshly-leafed trees — and that means increased exposure, 1/25 second, say, at *f*/6.3 or *f*/4.5. Not within the scope of a simple camera — unless you can place it on something firm, such as the edge of a box or table, and make a very short time exposure, about 1 second . . . or make a synchronized photoflash shot. But it's certainly a picture worth the effort.

70

Back-lighted pictures, and snaps in open shade, are easy — you merely increase the exposure, or toss in some extra light. Picture at left would be 1/50 second, *f*/8, on Kodak Verichrome or Kodak Plus-X Film. A reflector — such as a white sheet, newspaper, or white house wall — helps brighten the shadows. In deep shade, use a time exposure, or synchronized flash.

Here, reflections from the blanket and from Mother's face brighten up the shadow side of the baby's face.

small fry offer a picture every minute

The baby sunning himself in his play pen is a different proposition. Plenty of light there for easy snaps with any camera. And asleep or awake, chewing on a rattle, trying to put his foot in his mouth, he's picture material . . . the best.

Just now, the pup's trying to get into the pen, with the baby's help. How to show them both? A high-up camera position, with the camera aimed steeply downward, ought to do it nicely.

Now, put the pup inside, and they'll both try to get out — offering still more pictures.

But beware of fast motion if you're using a simple camera. Watch for pauses. They occur, even with babies and pups; and they help insure unblurred pictures.

71

Everybody's busy in these four snaps — so they are good. At left, picture is restricted to four simple elements: boy, paint, brush, and a background that helps the story. Right, a dark background shows up the action. In the boy-and-dog conference below, the two dark profiles are neatly silhouetted against a simple background. And good action, at lower right, makes the picture.

let's step along—there's much to cover

In the back yard, a game of junior horseshoes is in process. Action's too fast for a simple camera, but you can get shots of the young players making ready for a toss, or measuring a close one at the peg, which are every bit as interesting as the fast action.

A game of marbles, too, in case any of Johnny's cronies come over, will offer good material for backyard sports shots.

The wash is on the line — or being hung out. Is it picture material? Well, shots of someone hanging out the family wash *have* won prizes in picture contests. Prizes or no, it's an interesting bit of family activity to brighten up any album.

How to picture it — white laundry against a blue sky? Here's where your K-2 Filter comes in. Slip it over the lens; it will darken the blue sky a bit, and the sunlit clothes will stay white.

At right, a yellow filter helps keep pleasing sky tones. Below, a high camera and background of deep shadow yield a clean-cut portrayal of washday action. Around home, watch for humorous sidelights — such as the doll on the clothesline.

Backyard games are worth-while picture material. At right, the strong side lighting from a late afternoon sun adds pictorial interest to a very simple scene.

snapshots in the garden, too

If you are too late to picture the spading and seeding of this year's garden, there will be other pictures coming along all season; shots of the weeding, cultivating, harvesting . . . and, in the kitchen, all the canning and freezing operations. Every phase is a part of the family history, and it's all picture material.

So is every other phase of activity in the yard, the dozens of things yet unmentioned — backyard picnics and wiener-roasts, flowers and the cutting of flowers, lawn-sprinkling and fun with the hose, other summer games; in the autumn, the colorful trees and the leaf-raking and bonfires; in the winter, the building of the first snow man, and the house decorated with its Christmas dress . . .

But let's move inside.

73

More action — and so, good pictures. Left, a high camera was best; at right, camera was lowered to change the background. Below, left, the boy's clasped hands and rapt pose add a delightful touch; below, right, action was caught at the perfect moment. Curve of the hose has a pleasing pictorial quality.

first stop, obviously—the nursery

Here's one room that's full of pictures whenever it's occupied. If sunshine streams into a big nursery window, that's the finest of light sources. Place the baby's crib or play pen or blanket in the sunlight. On his shadow side, place a reflector (such as a white sheet) or a photoflood lamp, 5 or 6 feet from him, to brighten the shadow areas. Load your camera with Kodak Super-XX Film, and focus it for a short distance, 4 or 5 feet, or put on a Kodak Close-Up Attachment.

Then give the baby his favorite toys, and let him play. Wait for clear action, good expressions — but let him alone. No need to enumerate things that will yield pictures; almost anything he does offers a new treasure for the album.

With the baby in direct sun from a large window, and Kodak Super-XX Film in a simple-lens camera, regular snapshot exposures can be made. Set other cameras at 1/100 second and $f/11$, or 1/50 and $f/16$. Keep the camera at the right distance from the baby, and it's as simple as snapshooting outdoors.

74

Let the sunshine in — and nursery snapshots are easy. Of course, it's not quite as bright as outdoors, so use a faster film — Kodak Super-XX. Provide a toy to evoke good expressions — and use a Kodak Portra Lens or Close-up Attachment for close-range pictures. They're more satisfying.

Use a reflector on the shadow side, to obtain clear bright shadows. ➡ And try some very-close studies of the baby's hands, as at left.

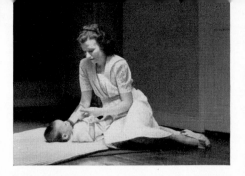

Natural "spotlighting" adds interest to pictures.
Above, a skylight was the light source; at right,
sunlight through a window served beautifully.

at night, it's almost as easy

Photoflood lights bother a baby only if they're too close, or if he
sees them against a background of shadow. For night snaps,
place the play pen or crib close to a light-colored wall. Direct
one Reflector Photoflood light *straight up*, to illuminate the
room ceiling. Place another Reflector Photoflood alongside the
play pen, about 3 feet from floor level, and point it down at an
angle so that part of the light reaches the baby directly, and part
of it reflects from the wall beyond him, illuminating his shadow
side. Load the camera with Kodak Super-XX Film. With a simple-lens camera, make snapshot exposures. If your camera has
f-markings, use 1/25 second at $f/11$, or 1/50 at $f/8$.

If you can dispense with the crib or pen, so much the better.
Then, instead of shooting from above, you can bring the camera
down near the baby's own eye level, which is the best viewpoint
for most baby close-ups.

75

High camera for this. ➡

⬇ Low camera for this.

Camera down
low for this
one too — it
makes a dif-
ference. ➡

You'll treasure snaps such as these — far more than any "formal" pictures.

in the bathroom, the same setup

This same night setup is also excellent for shots in the average light-walled bathroom — snaps of the baby being bathed, weighed, and so on — because the light-colored walls help diffuse a soft, gentle illumination that's practically perfect for baby pictures.

Elsewhere, too, this smallest of small fry will grant you many a picture chance. No need to restrict him to toys. To provide variety, he'll be happy to listen to father's watch ticking, to chew up the morning paper, or pull all the new magazines to pieces. Even though his table manners are a bit shaky, he won't mind your snapping pictures at mealtime. He'll be glad to play with any family pet that's safe for him to handle. And every one of these — along with other activities — yields new pictures for the book.

76   Now, let's get on with our tour.

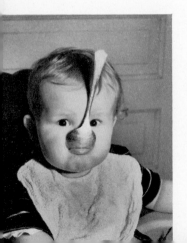

◄Rely on synchronized flash for quick shots of spontaneous action — such as Butch's snack-time antics.

For pictures that can be partly or fully planned, either flood or flash will do. ➡

pictures in the living room

New living room furniture and decorations call for new pictures. Dad in his favorite chair, with a book or the evening paper, is at his photogenic best. Party activities are always worth picturing – and easy, too, in these days of synchronized flash. The fireplace is a natural spot for family group pictures – and when a family is growing up fast, such pictures shouldn't be skimped.

Picturing a room by daylight is not difficult. Usually a corner position is best for the camera, preferably a corner that does not face toward brilliantly lighted windows. Put the camera on a table, or other firm support, and stop the lens down to *f*/16. If the room lighting appears "spotty," with dark corners, place one or two photoflood lamps outside the camera's field of view, but

how to get everything sharp

When you picture a scene or situation, you often want every detail sharp. Judicious focusing – and proper choice of the lens opening – will help you accomplish that.

Take a practical example, a group at the piano. The nearest person is about 6½ feet from the camera; the farthest, about 10 feet. So, you need a "depth of field" of about 3½ feet.

Do you set the camera for 6 feet, or 10 feet? Neither. Set it at 8 feet, and close the lens down to *f*/11. With the average hand camera that takes 2¼x3¼-inch pictures, your zone of acceptable sharpness now covers the group. (If you're only planning to get album-size prints or small enlargements, the zone of reasonably sharp focus is even wider.)

The table below shows depths at other distances, and other lens openings, for practically any amateur camera that takes 2¼x3¼ pictures. A depth scale is built right into some of the modern Kodak cameras.

Distance Camera Is Set For	Size Of Subject Covered	FIELD DEPTH—IN FEET—FOR ACCEPTABLE DETAIL				
		f/3.5	*f*/5.6	*f*/8	*f*/11	*f*/22
100 feet	62′ x 100′	56 to inf.	42 to inf.	34 to inf.	26 to inf.	14¾ to inf.
50 feet	28′ x 41′	36 to 83	29 to 200	25 to inf.	21 to inf.	13 to inf.
25 feet	14′ x 20′	20½ to 31	18½ to 38	16¾ to 48	14¾ to 91	10½ to inf.
15 feet	8¼′ x 12⅙′	13⅓ to 17½	12½ to 19½	11¾ to 22½	10½ to 28	8 to inf.
10 feet	5½′ x 8′	9¼ to 11¼	8¾ to 11¾	8½ to 12½	7¾ to 14	6½ to 22
8 feet	4⅓′ x 6⅓′	7½ to 8½	7¼ to 9	7 to 9½	6½ to 10⅓	5½ to 14½
6 feet	3¼′ x 4⅔′	5¾ to 6⅓	5⅔ to 6⅔	5⅓ to 6¾	5⅙ to 7¼	4½ to 9½
5 feet	2⅔′ x 3¾′	4⅚ to 5¼	4⅔ to 5⅓	4½ to 5½	4⅓ to 5⅚	3⅚ to 7¼
4 feet	2′ x 3′	3⅚ to 4⅙	3¾ to 4¼	3⅔ to 4⅓	3⅔ to 4½	3⅓ to 5¼
3½ feet	1⅔′ x 2½′	3½ to 3½	3⅓ to 3⅔	3⅓ to 3¾	3¼ to 3⅚	2⅚ to 4⅓

Exposure for this attractive bed-room scene, 1/10 second at *f*/8, Kodak Verichrome Film, bright sunny day. ↓

↑ For this pleasant interior view, 1/5 second, *f*/5.6, Kodak Super-XX Film. That would be about 2 seconds at *f*/16. Note the interesting shadow pattern on the floor; it breaks up a rather monotonous area of tone.

in such positions that they soften the deep shadows. On a sunny day, if the room has two or more windows and the walls are medium in color, a time exposure of 8 to 10 seconds at *f*/16 will generally give good results on Kodak Verichrome Film or Kodak Plus-X Film. On Kodak Super-XX Film, at *f*/16, try 4 or 5 seconds. The same exposure times, on those films, will serve if you are using a box camera or other simple-lens camera. On a *cloudy* day, make the exposure about three times as long.

These exposure suggestions are approximate — because rooms vary greatly. But the results on your first shots will serve as a guide in later exposures.

78

Keeping up with the Sunday comics is important — and a good picture, easy with synchronized flash. ↓

flash shots, and party pictures

At night, it's easy to picture a room by synchronized photoflash. With Kodak Super-XX Film in your camera, lens set at $f/11$, and shutter at 1/50 second, a No. 5 photoflash lamp will illuminate a room 12 to 20 feet long, when the lamp and camera are at one end. If the room is 30 feet long, use $f/5.6$. To picture a 12-to-20-foot room with an SM photoflash lamp and Kodak Super-XX Film, set the lens at $f/8$; use $f/4.5$ if the room is 30 feet long. If you're using a simple-lens camera, and the room is longer than 15 feet, just bring the camera and flash forward until they're not more than 15 feet from the end of the room you're picturing.

Both Kodak Verichrome Film and Kodak Plus-X Film are excellent for flash work. With either one, when picturing a 12-to-20-foot room by No. 5 photoflash, use 1/50 at $f/8$; with SM flash, 1/50 at $f/5.6$.

All these exposures are for light-walled rooms. Dark walls, of course, call for shorter distances or larger lens openings.

Synchronized flash is by far the best light for pictures of an indoor party. But avoid general shots of a roomful of people. Small groups — such as a foursome at bridge, or a couple by the fireplace — make a more interesting record. These are, naturally, taken at shorter camera-to-subject ranges, so consult your Flash Kodaguide for accurate exposure information. Basic exposures for close-range pictures, on any of the popular Kodak black-and-white or color films, by either flood or flash, are given on Page 160.

79

◄ Nothing like music to liven up the old homestead. A flash shot.

For this, a single light, directly overhead. Boy's face is lighted by reflections from the table. ➡

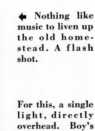

y rip-roaring pillow-fights in your album?
was easy—1/100 second, $f/4$, Kodak Super-XX
two No. 2 flood lamps in reflectors.

Tuck a flood or flash lamp back in the fireplace — and these shots are easy.

fireplace shots can be faked

With time exposures, pictures can be taken by real firelight. However, it's sometimes difficult for people to hold still during the exposure. So, instead of having a real fire, just hide a photoflood lamp back in a corner of the fireplace. Then, on Kodak Super-XX Film, you'll be able to take snapshot exposures (1/50 second at $f/6.3$ when a Reflector Photoflood, or a No. 2 photoflood in a reflector, is about 5 feet from your subjects' faces). To keep the firelight effect, dim the room lights.

For portraits of the family at home, use either flood or flash. Suppose you want to picture Father reading, or Sis knitting in a corner of the sofa by the light of a table lamp or floor lamp. To obtain a pleasant, natural effect, put a No. 1 photoflood lamp in the house lamp, and place a Reflector Photoflood lamp about four feet from the subject for general illumination. You can then take snapshot exposures, even with a simple-lens camera, on Kodak Super-XX Film. One caution: since photoflood lamps become very hot, don't let them touch a lamp shade of cloth or paper, or other inflammable objects.

color shots indoors and out

Any of the pictures suggested in this chapter can be taken in full color. For daylight shots, remember to use Kodachrome Film, or Kodacolor Film, *Daylight Type*. For shots indoors after dark,

⬆ When Johnny
goes to work on
the new car, his
pride and enthusi-
asm are well worth
picturing. Plan to
keep part of your
family picture sto-
ry in color.

Color is right, ➡
too, when new pets
are being wel-
comed. In this ap-
pealing picture,
note that the sun
was back of the
camera, for a flat
lighting. In most
color pictures, col-
or contrast is suf-
ficient; you do not
need light-and-
shade contrast.

81

Kodachrome or Kodacolor Film, *Type A,* is used with regular flood and flash lamps. No filter is required for photoflood shots; in flash shots, a filter should be used with most lamps (see the table on Page 160). Flash shots (without filters) may be taken on daylight films by means of *blue-bulb* flash lamps.

Remember that, in any color shot, the lights must be placed at accurate distances for correct exposure — so follow carefully the data in your Snapshot Kodaguide.

the kitchen is a busy place

Kitchen activities yield marvelously interesting pictures — especially close-ups. Everybody, of course, remembers to snap the Thanksgiving or Christmas turkey as it comes out of the oven. But slip a Kodak Close-Up Attachment or Portra Lens over the lens of your camera, and move in for a snap of Grandmother's hands as she rolls out a batch of biscuits . . . picture her pie-making technique as she critically trims off the surplus crust or places neat strips across the top . . . catch a pattern shot of the dishes rhythmically stacked in the wire tray . . . nip out to the back porch some morning and focus on the milk bottles standing fresh and white in the early sun . . . and you'll be working in a vein that has brought amateur photographers many a blue ribbon in exhibitions or contests. Further, you'll be piling up treasures for your collection . . . shots that are intimate, different, and a stimulating challenge to your picture-taking skill.

82

At right, a flood lamp highlighted the subject's hair; 1/50 second, *f*/8, Kodak Super-XX Film.➡ Below, bottles and shadows make a pattern picture.

Sunshine made a good "spotlight" for this interesting close-up of hands in action. ⬇

Every season is a camera season

... And each one has its individual picture opportunities — just waiting. At left, installation of the new bird house is smartly pictured against a filtered sky. At right, shadows on the snow yield an appealing snap for the children's album. At bottom of page, meetings of young and old always offer appealing picture situations.

We started this "right around home" chapter on a sunny spring day — but at home, every season is a camera season. Summer means garden work, flowers (and there's a special chapter about flower pictures later on), preparation of picnic lunches, young- 83

Every season is a color season, too — even the months you think are colorless and gray. Above, Winter's mood is aptly captured on Kodachrome Film, in subtle harmonies of white, gray, and blue shadows, with just a touch of evergreen.

In contrast to Winter's quiet harmonies, consider the brilliance of Spring, and the riot of Summer's flowering — gold, green, bright reds, lush purples, and all the rest of the rainbow. Your color camera can always be busy around home. ↓

Picturing interiors in color is a simple matter. Best time is after dark. Arrange two or more flood lamps to produce a soft, evenly-distributed lighting. Then measure the distance from the lights to the far end walls—and your Snapshot Kodaguide will give you the correct exposure for those lamp-to-subject distances. For example, with Kodachrome Film, Type A, and two No. 2 photofloods 13 feet from the part of the room you're picturing, basic exposure will be 1 second at $f/6.3$. Make sure your lights do not reflect from mirrors or other shiny surfaces. Proper films are Kodachrome, Type A, or Kodacolor, Type A. If you use them indoors by day, take care to exclude all daylight. For other distances, see Page 160.

85

When picturing action, remember to step up your shutter speed (see Page 52). Here, the subjects are moving toward the camera—so motion is reduced.

Photo lights aren't needed in all cases. Here, the candles alone are best; try 1/5 second, *f*/4.5, on Kodak Super-XX Film.

sters starting out on Boy Scout and Girl Scout hikes, lawn spraying (and its accompanying play, with the small fry in bathing suits), and many other activities — all worth picturing. Maybe the house gets a new coat of paint; *that* must be pictured for posterity. Birthdays and anniversaries — with their parties and gifts — arrive almost any time. In late summer, there are bits of the garden harvest to photograph . . . in autumn, more harvesting, canning, leaf-raking, bonfires, Thanksgiving preparations, and the gorgeous round of autumn color . . . in winter, snow to shovel or to give the Christmas sled its first tryout, and frost on the windowpanes, to be pictured as the morning sun shines through, or as the children write their names across it . . . and when spring comes again, blossoms to picture, and April showers, and the spring tune-up for Buster's bicycle. These, and a thousand other things — the pets and their antics, a new batch of pups or kittens now and then, the taking down of screens and putting up of storm windows on the first frosty week end, Junior all dressed up for his first trip to school . . .

Around home, anything is a picture, any time of the year — and it all belongs in the family's snapshot history.

86

Summer's harvests and Winter's icicles both belong in your history of home events. For the icicle picture, 1 second at *f*/16, with a No. 2 photoflood lamp.

Pictures
about town

THERE ARE HUNDREDS of pictures in your home town — whether it's a village or a metropolis of millions. Form the habit of taking your camera for exploratory tours around town, and you'll bring home many a shot to add spice to your collection.

Pick up your camera, slip a roll of film into it, *drop a spare roll in your pocket,* and we'll take a trip around town to spot some of these pictorial opportunities.

architecture—and your house

At the front gate of your home, pause and turn around. You'll be picturing buildings, and your own home is one of the most important. Right here, we should tick off a few pointers on architectural photography.

There's a best time of day for pictures of any building. It usually occurs when the sun slants across the front of the building, tracing a crisp outline of shadow along each window, clapboard, or other architectural feature. Snap your picture at that hour, and it will be better.

87

Summer and winter comparison pictures — taken from the same position — are nice features for your "at home" album. And don't forget autumn color!

Above, a pleasant view of a pleasant street—all the better because it was taken from a well-chosen position, with the camera pointed across the street at about a 45-degree angle. The same angle would be desirable for an individual "portrait" of any one of the houses.

It's not necessary to show the entire house ➡ in every shot. A pleasant walk — an attractive doorway — can be a picture in its own right.

There's always a best viewpoint, too — and it's seldom "front and center." Step up or down the street a little way, study the house through your view finder, and see if the "quartering view" isn't more pleasing. If there are trees along the street, step back a bit more, and see if you can utilize an overhanging branch to make a pleasant leafy arch above the house. Perhaps there's a gate through which the house can be "framed" in an attractive manner; such foreground framing adds greatly to a picture.

Another important point is camera *elevation*. Avoid tilting the camera upward toward a building, for that makes the vertical lines converge — and the structure seems to taper upward. Step up on the bumper of a parked car, or your neighbor's porch across the street; you'll gain a little extra elevation, and can keep the camera more nearly level.

tall buildings are different

Downtown, or in the city, if you picture tall slender skyscrapers or high-spired churches, it may be impossible to avoid tilting the camera. In that event, it's often interesting to point the camera steeply upward, to obtain an exaggerated tapering effect which suggests enormous height.

Not only when bright flowers are on sale on the streets—but at every other season—there's plenty of color to be pictured around town. Take color film along on your picture tours.

Seek a natural "frame" for your pictures of buildings. Foliage, or a gateway, can often be useful. Each of these three pictures shows effective framing — obtained through careful choice of camera position.

Suppose we pick a route downtown that takes us through one of the city parks. Near the entrance, there's a wading pool — an ideal spot for snapping pictures of children at play. Slip your Kodak Lens Hood on the camera, and try a few back-lighted or "against-the-light" shots. The ripples on the water, and the splashing spray, will take on added brilliance when the sun is somewhat ahead of the camera.

Pause at the swimming pool, too. Here are not only graceful and skilled divers, but also the inevitable clowns. For high-diving shots, try a position close below the tower, aim upward at an angle, and show the diver against the sky. For swimmers, use a high viewpoint, angling downward. Don't overlook the beginners, pumping along with the aid of old inner-tubes or water wings . . . nor the sun-bathers scattered about the edge of the pool. And don't forget to use a shutter speed fast enough for the action (see Page 52 and Chapter 17).

the zoo is a camera fan's gold mine

Next, let's say we come to the city zoo. Even if it isn't a big one, it will be a gold mine for pictures, both pictorial and humorous. Every animal has its individual personality. Some are worth photographing for their sheer beauty. Others will certainly re-

At the pool, remember that the sky is usually the ➡ best of all outdoor backgrounds. Slip the yellow filter on the lens, and keep it there for most shots. For diving pictures, a low camera position, angling up, is generally the best choice.

To show activity on the pier or float, try a high camera position, angling down. This is also the best angle, as a rule, when you picture groups in action on a playing field, court, rink, or other arena. ⬇

⬆ Watch for individual, "human interest" opportunities—such as this young sailor.

⬅ Keep an eye out, too, for the odd and unusual. Who'd ever think of taking a diving picture like this? But somebody did—and it's good.

Natural, isn't it, to test the water before you wade in? And because it is such a natural act, it made a charming picture —worthy of anybody's album. ⬇

mind you of some person you know; still others will provide amusing antics for the camera to record.

Don't worry about the cage bars and wires. Where necessary, let them show. If you're using a large lens opening, such as $f/6.3$ or $f/4.5$, and the animal isn't dangerous, you can put your lens right up to a wire cage, and shoot. Even if a wire is right in front of the lens, it will be so far out of focus that it just disappears.

Sometimes you can't get close enough to an animal to fill your film satisfactorily, but don't worry about that; the section on making enlargements (Chapter 20) tells you how to pick out a part of a negative, and enlarge it to the size you desire.

92

anyone you know?

 "Unaccustomed as Ah am to public speaking, Ah would merely like to re-mahk briefly . . ."

"I won't go. I simply ➡ won't go. I need a new permanent, and I haven't got a thing to wear."

⬅ "They framed me, Judge!"

"Mr. Chairman and gentlemen, the Nominating Committee offer this report —" ⬇

◄ At any zoo, elephants offer rewarding material. Study the neat, effective grouping in this story-telling shot.

Good action, natural ➤ framing, and strong side-lighting contribute great-ly to the effect of this pleasant little picture.

and when the circus or carnival comes...

Start when the show begins to unload. ➤ A high viewpoint is best for general views of unloading activities.

Capture all the small sidelights — such as this. It could make a good cover enlarge-ment for a circus album. ⬇

For a priceless picture story — take a child to the circus with you. ➤

Dramatize the rides with an up-angle and sky. ⬇

High viewpoint and good ➡ action help make this picture. Note that the rows of flowers cross the picture "on the bias"— a diagonal nearly always lends extra zest to a picture.

⬅ The dark figure in a spot of sun is very effective — it creates a "center of interest" for this quiet, charming scene in the park.

For close-ups in the ➡ public gardens — remember to take your Portra Lens along.

public gardens are interesting

If your park includes a public garden, you'll find material for another field day — interesting vistas and bits of landscape, and flower varieties you don't have in your flower beds at home. If the public garden is unusually good, you may use it to start a collection of color slides or color prints, portraying the varieties that interest you most. Practical details of technique are in the chapter on flower pictures.

butcher, baker, candlestick maker

Suppose we leave the park now, and stroll down to the shopping center or business section. Here's a treasure land for any camera

An alert eye will spot picture material everywhere. As you seek subjects, try for a novel approach — a treatment that's "just a little bit different." This picture gains in naturalness and dramatic value because the car is used to 'frame' the bridge ahead.

fan who's interested in people and activity. In front of his store, a grocer carefully arranges his displays, and hangs up a bunch of bananas — perhaps with a small boy watching, admiringly or hopefully. At a construction job, the "sidewalk superintendents" observe critically, while a power shovel scoops up great bites of earth, or a riveter or mason deftly does his stuff. By the curb, a scissors-grinder spins his foot-powered wheel, or judicially tests the edge of a newly honed blade. Delivery trucks disgorge vast trays of freshly baked pies, and husky loaders hoist new refrigerators or bathtubs into other vans. Every moment of these and a thousand other activities offers you another picture.

To capture these pictures, learn to handle your camera in a casual, unobtrusive manner. Keep the lens and shutter set for correct exposure and normal action — say, 1/100 second at $f/8$ when you're using Kodak Verichrome or Kodak Plus-X Film. Focus for an average distance — say 15 feet, which will enable you to shoot anything from about 12 to 20 feet without resetting. Then you're all ready for shots of most street activities.

practice quick view-finding

Learn to use your view finder quickly and surely. It's merely a matter of practice — and of deciding promptly what you want in the picture. With a bit of experience, you'll know just about how large an area your camera will cover at any given distance from a subject.

95

men at work

← Here's good action, caught at the right moment. It's worth studying.

Dramatic back lighting lends interest to this study of a carpenter's hands. ↓

Some cameras — such as the Kodak Reflex and Kodak Duaflex Cameras—are especially suited for unobtrusive shooting. You can face partly away from your subject, point the camera to your left or right, look down into the finder to frame the subject—and shoot. Most of the time, if your subject notices the camera at all, he'll think you're shooting in the direction you're facing.

a bit of law to remember

Unposed pictures, snapped without the subject's knowledge, tend to be natural and realistic. However, such snaps cannot be used for commercial purposes, nor entered in certain snapshot contests. It's a good idea, after you have your picture, to introduce yourself to the subject, and offer to send him a print for himself. That puts matters on a friendly, straightforward basis; and later on, if you want to enter the picture in a contest, you can go to the subject and ask for his permission in the form of a written "release."

You'll often find, after you have introduced yourself to your

96

The boom and cables draw your eyes straight
to the figure outlined against the sky. ➡

Stacked material yields a "pattern" picture. ⬇

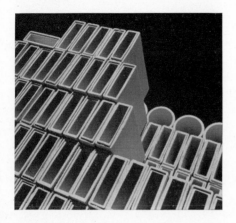

subject, that he'll be happy to help you take other pictures —
showing bits of action you may have missed, or permitting you
to choose a better angle or a closer view. In this way, you can
often make a complete "picture story" of an interesting street
activity — a half dozen or more good shots instead of just one
shot. The complete story is always better.

high up and looking down

Before leaving the business section, see if you can't locate a
second-story or third-story vantage point above a busy corner.
Try a few snaps of the heavy traffic, the traffic cop, the street
crowds. Plan to come back sometime in late afternoon, when the
sun is low and streaming down the street, making long shadows
and interesting patterns. The high position provides a new and
distinctive angle for your pictures.

Remember this, too, when you want to picture a parade. Get
well above it, and shoot downward. Your pictures will be much
clearer, more interesting, than if you shoot the whole parade

from street level. Even a moderate elevation — such as the steps of a public building — is a help in making street shots.

nooks, corners, and byways

Places you rarely visit are good spots to look for pictures — because everything is new and interesting. But don't let the novelty mislead you; shoot with discrimination — and keep in mind the requirements of lighting and arrangement that we covered in the chapter on "Good and Better Pictures."

Try the open-air market, the public docks, factory and industrial areas. Each has a fund of superb picture material. Probe into narrow back alleys and side streets; you may find atmospheric effects, and tumble-down buildings with the charm of the old and unexpected. Look for things of historic interest; it's an absorbing hobby to make a picture collection based on local history. The town's oldest building, its oldest church, outmoded

public buildings that have been abandoned for modern structures, an old fountain or public well, an old hitching post cast in the form of a boy holding an iron ring, quaint and whimsical bits of architecture, plaques that tell the story of some memorable spot or building—these are all material for such a collection. Observe shop signs; you may find old signs with queer lettering, full of odd ornaments and curlicues, that was fashionable a generation or two ago. They're well worth picturing.

The story of your city's past makes interesting pictures now. The story of your city as it is today will have historic interest tomorrow. Each picture will grow in value as time passes, will take on added attraction for yourself, your family, and your friends.

keep your camera with you, and ready

Make it your practice, whenever possible, to keep your camera with you. You'll gain many a picture worth having. You may   **99**

chance on a fire, or some other emergency, that yields pictures of pictorial or practical value. When you're driving, keep the camera on the seat beside you. (Don't, by the way, keep it in the glove compartment; it's too hot in there on a sunny day.) In the event of an accident, a ready camera may have immense, immediate value.

And cultivate an alert eye. Watch constantly for picture opportunities. They're all around you, all the time, at home or away from home — and you need only learn to recognize them.

young men
about town

Here's a bit of humor ➡ — and a dash of exciting drama — straight from the public park. Note the expression of the top man on this "totem pole." Wherever there's activity — work or play — you'll find such opportunities. You don't need unusual subjects — it's what you do with everyday subjects that counts. Look for the critical moment — the "different" angle — the expression or action that tells a story — and you'll get good pictures everywhere.

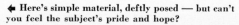
← Here's simple material, deftly posed — but can't you feel the subject's pride and hope?

Note the musician's soulful eyes, and the rapt audience. Here's true, genuine "human interest"— a snapshot to grace any collection. ⬇

Pictures
at school

IF YOU'RE ATTENDING SCHOOL, you need a camera. Now is the time to make a pictorial record of your friends and schoolmates, and the activities and school events, on which you will look back with pleasure in later years. If you do not make such a record now, you can never make it at all.

School is a busy place. Every minute is filled; every hour offers a new activity. And each of these activities is material for pictures.

something doing every minute

Take a quick inventory — and you'll find an amazing number of things you want to remember. Friends in the study hall, or outside in breaks or recesses between classes. Experiments in the laboratory — a wonderful place for pictorial shots of expressions   **101**

Synchronized flash makes pictures easy anywhere — lab, study hall, gym, class. But ask permission first!

and apparatus. Gymnasium activities. Student council meetings. The school newspaper staff at work. Orchestra and band rehearsals — not just general shots, but also close-ups of individual players. School parades. Athletics — football, baseball, and basketball practice; track meets; tennis, badminton, and others. Rehearsals and preparations for class plays — including preparation of scenery, shots of the cast and activity backstage, and pictures of crucial moments on stage. Snaps of favorite teachers and coaches. School buildings — between classes, when students are moving from building to building. The list of things to keep is practically endless.

make your own yearbook

Many schools publish yearbooks — a fine idea — but with your own camera, you can create an additional yearbook that is per-

Student council, plays, the snack bar, jalopies—all give you picture material.

sonal to *you*. In it, you can put the schoolmates and activities that interest you most — dozens of pictures, a true picture story of your school year.

And if you're at school away from home, your camera permits you to send snapshots home — showing the new friends you have made, and the activities in which you are taking part.

equipment need not be complex

Excellent work can be done with simple cameras. The camera should, however, be equipped for flash shots, so that you can take snaps indoors quickly, without setting up special lights. A Kodak Duaflex Camera, with Flasholder, is a good, moderately priced choice. Among the faster-lensed cameras, a Kodak Reflex or Kodak Tourist Camera is excellent. Miniature cameras, such as a Kodak Flash Bantam Camera, or a Kodak 35 Camera, have

The yearbook editor will be looking for sidelights and sports action — and snaps of every other activity!

At school dances — and when dusk catches a late game — your flash camera will insure good pictures.

fine fast lenses and flash shutters — and will enable you to take full-color transparencies on Kodachrome Film, as well as black-and-white snaps. (The other, larger cameras are full-color cameras too; they accept Kodacolor Film, which yields full-color prints.)

Incidentally, a camera and flash attachment make a fine graduation gift, for anyone finishing grade or high school; and for others whose school record is good enough to justify a special year-end gift. Such a gift is useful in any later school or college term; indeed, no student should go off to college without a camera of his own.

104

A camera keeps your school memories — up to the very end.

There's color too, in school and after school, at every season.

Pictures
in the country

WHENEVER YOU GO OUT into the country, take your camera along. Use it as an artist uses his sketch book, to jot down the interesting, unusual, or beautiful things you see.

Even the shortest rural excursion will reveal a treasure of picture opportunities. It really isn't so much what you see, as how you handle it. Or, as the professional might say, the secret is in your manipulation of picture material.

bicycle jaunts, picnics

Consider a simple bike ride, in a park or through a stretch of countryside. You could take a few casual shots, without much thought — and you'd have an album record of sorts. But instead, apply a little planning, like this:

As your group prepares to start out, get a shot of one member
106 putting the picnic lunch into a bicycle hamper; get another shot

Silhouette at right shows good planning; beginners' antics, below, can be predicted. Keep camera low for sky background.

of someone putting on trouser guards, or folding up the bicycle stand. Let one person start off down the road, while another stands ready to mount; snap the picture with the standing person in the foreground, and the other fairly well down the road. When you come to a large tree, at the brow of a hill, silhouette your companions against the skyline, with the tree framing the top of the picture. As you approach an interesting curve, with trees casting shadows across the road, spurt ahead and photograph the rest of the group as they round the curve toward you. If you pass by a pond or quiet stream, let two or three of your friends stand at the edge with their bikes, while you cross to the far side and picture their reflections in the water.

And at the picnic ground, capture interesting bits of action that tell a story — spreading the cloth, unpacking the lunch, kindling a fire, someone serving food, and so on.

Such planned shooting — with a definite idea or novel touch for each shot — will give you real pictures, instead of just casual snaps. It takes practically no extra effort, and the results are much more satisfying.

107

Reflections at right create a more interesting picture; and observe how subjects stand out against the simple background of grass and sky. Roadway, below, crosses picture in a pleasing diagonal curve, and figures are nicely placed.

Color in the country has many moods. In this pleasing back-lighted shot, note how the girl's face picks up warm yellow reflections from the autumn leaves. Synchronized flash, with blue-bulb lamps and daylight-type film, can often be used to advantage in situations such as this.

Study the action and grouping of the subjects in the picture below. Such snaps cannot be "posed" — but with practice, you will learn to gauge a situation quickly, pick the correct camera position promptly, and anticipate the "perfect moment." Experience makes your judgment quick and sure.

⬆️There are several lessons in this striking autumn landscape. Note, first, the many horizontal or gently sloping lines; these contribute greatly to the feeling of rural peace. Note, next, the warmth of the yellow afternoon sun on the golden stubble, and the rich red of the barns; these warm colors lend a sense of comfort and cheer. Note also how the cloud shadow on the far hill echoes the dark bar of foreground shadow — snugly closing in the little valley and its pleasant homestead.

Color film often "sees" more accurately than your eye. This charming bit of winter landscape, at right, is a good example. Most of us think shadows are neutral in color—but the truth is, they're neutral only under a gray or hazy sky. Snow shadows under a blue sky are definitely blue — almost as blue as the sky itself — and Kodachrome Film has sensitively picked up this color reflection, perfectly capturing the mood of the winter scene.

In the country, as in the city, seek a natural "frame" for your picture subjects, as above. And in picturing people, catch the moments of spontaneous fun. ➡

pictures of campfires, too

On any rural jaunt that includes a campfire, pictures of the fire with the group around it are essential. Shots after dark are even more interesting than the daytime campfire snaps, and with short time exposures, they can be taken by firelight alone.

Too, if your camera has a flash shutter or a flash synchronizer, you can snap pictures of individuals or groups after dark as easily as in the daytime. Even with simple cameras, flash snaps can be taken outdoors at ranges up to 15 or 20 feet between the flash lamp and subject. You'll find additional details in the chapter on "Pictures After Dark."

110

For the after-dark beach shot, below, the camera was set for "time" — and a flash lamp discharged in a hand unit such as the inexpensive Kodak Photo Flasher.

When you picture scenic views, include a foreground —a figure, shadow, or frame of foliage. Let the person look at the scene, as shown here; not at the camera.

landscapes are pictorial material

Rural landscapes offer tempting opportunities for pictorial shots. The landscape need not be immense or breath-taking. Look for a pleasant glade, a small pool or waterfall, a tree beside a curving path. Such material is easier to organize into a pleasing arrangement – and it yields intimate pictures, full of quiet charm.

Next to subject matter, arrangement and lighting are most important. You can "rearrange" a landscape simply by changing your camera position – left or right, to bring foreground material into better relation with the distant parts of the scene; higher up or lower down, to achieve a more favorable viewpoint.

vistas, foregrounds, and clouds

Foreground material nearly always lends depth to a scenic view. If you're picturing a valley, from a hilltop, don't stand at the very edge of the hill. Back up, and include a tree, or a person admiring the distant view. If there are several trees, create a vista by "framing" the view between two or more trees with overhanging foliage.

Clouds usually improve a landscape. A color filter will help retain them, when the sky beyond is blue. For normal effects, use a yellow Kodak Wratten K-2 Filter with either panchromatic or orthochromatic film. For "strong" effects – brilliant white

For realism in a campfire scene, put your camera a firm support, and make a time exposure by the ht of the campfire. Or, let one of the group con- l a flash lamp, and set it off at your signal

Bird studies are a delightful field of specialization, if you're nature-minded; and color films have brought new value to this phase of the camera hobby. This Kodachrome Film study of a Cedar Waxwing at the nest is an example of what can be done. Sketch at right shows a simple feeding-station setup for your lawn; the board with perch should face south, to catch the sun most of the day. Camera can be fitted with a magnetic or "solenoid" release, with wires leading away to a convenient point of concealment for you. The same remote-control release is used when you picture birds in their native woodland.

For startling, dramatic landscape effects — try Kodak Infrared Film, with a red (Kodak Wratten A) filter. Skies show up rich and dark; clouds are brilliant white. Evergreen foliage records very dark, but the leaves of deciduous trees show white, as here. The basic exposure for infrared shots outdoors is 1/25 second at *f*/4.5. Picture at right was 1/25, *f*/6.3.

clouds and very dark or black sky — use a red Kodak Wratten A Filter with panchromatic or infrared film (but *not* with an orthochromatic film).

mist, haze, and atmosphere

Mist or haze helps give atmospheric quality to a landscape. Filters will not penetrate mist, because it is white. Bluish haze can be reduced by using a filter such as the Kodak Wratten A or G Filter, when you wish to show the distant landscape with greater clarity.

Soft, atmospheric quality can also be achieved by placing a Kodak Pictorial Diffusion Disk over the camera lens. In certain intimate landscapes and farm scenes, the effect is extremely pleasing; sunlit objects appear to glow with a soft radiance. In certain other landscapes, you will want as much crisp, sharp detail as possible; for these, diffusion should not be used. Make your choice after you decide how you want to interpret the scene.

lighting also for depth

Shadows are important in landscapes; and regular behind-the-camera lighting seldom yields best results. Keep your Kodak Lens Hood handy, and seek scenic material that is side-lighted or back-lighted, so that shadows cross the scene or fall *toward*

113

Morning mist or winter
moonlight — both are
picture material.

the camera. Utilize the lens hood so that direct sunshine will not strike the camera lens.

However, don't think that beautiful landscape pictures are reserved for sunny days. Many an interesting scenic has been captured on a wet day — or in the middle of a snowstorm. The subject matter and weather conditions are important — but it's what *you* do that really counts.

simplicity is the secret

As in other pictures, simplicity is essential to a good landscape shot. Select your position so as to exclude extraneous material — objects that don't harmonize with the rest of the scene. Try to compose the masses, tones, and lines to produce a pleasing, coherent arrangement. And don't let vast, open scenes mislead you; the *pictures* are usually discovered in small portions of such general scenes.

When a vast panorama spreads before you, and you want it all — make a panoramic picture, a series of shots that can be
114 mounted together in a strip. First, place your camera on a firm,

This is a two-picture panorama — two prints mounted to make one scene. ↓ They're moonlight shots — full moon, 30 minutes, f/8, Kodak Super-XX Film.

level support. Starting at the left side of the scene, take one picture. Turn the camera far enough so that the second picture will overlap about a quarter of the first (this gives you a margin for matching) and shoot again. Continue in this manner until you have pictured the whole scene. A camera support such as the Kodak Eye-Level Tripod, fitted with a Kodak Turn-Tilt Head, is ideal for this type of picture taking.

lines, masses, and proportions

In arranging scenes, there are several rules of good composition to be observed. Rarely should a horizon line cut squarely across the middle of the scene, for this divides the picture into uninteresting equal parts. Align the camera so it includes more sky than land — or, especially if there are people or other prominent elements in the foreground, more land than sky. If there is a road, pathway, or stream, let it enter the picture near a corner, and lead the eye diagonally to a central point of interest. Avoid masses of equal size, symmetrically placed; several small objects on one side will nicely balance a large object on the other side of the picture. Don't place the most important part of the scene in the exact center of your picture; dead center is nearly always the weakest spot.

Each kind of line has its own significance. Diagonal lines suggest liveliness and movement. Long level horizontal lines imply peace, calmness, and quiet. Tall vertical lines connote dignity, 115

Curving furrows lead the eye into this picture, up to the center of interest, the tractor. Strong side lighting brings out interesting texture and pattern in the plowed land. ➡

Broad pyramidal masses lend rugged stability to this cliff-top cottage picture.

and curving lines lend graceful quality. Combine them carefully, either for harmony or contrast, and your landscape pictures will achieve true beauty.

farm scenes and scenics

Landscape pictures need not consist wholly of trees and streams. A building — cottage, farmhouse, barn, or a mill — can often be used as the focal point or center of interest. Such buildings may be neat and well-tended, or dilapidated and picturesque; it does not matter, as long as they harmonize with the rest of the scene.

Farm activities are also welcome elements in many landscape shots. A team of horses or a tractor may serve either to punctuate the distant scene, or as foreground material. Sheep and cattle, grazing, lend a desirable touch of life to a scenic view.

116

Wrecked barn and wheel make an interesting pattern shot; and the rush to load the hay before the storm breaks is picture-worthy action. ➡

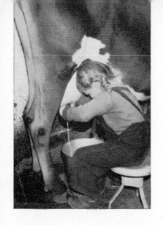

For the action picture of the young milk-maid, synchronized flash put the light where it was needed. Such everyday operations as this — and mealtime in the hen-yard, at right — will add variety to your album of rural pictures. Try a step-by-step sequence, too — showing the details of one or more activities.

close-ups on the farm, too

After you've taken your farm scenics from a distance, move in and get acquainted with the close-range picture opportunities. Any farm activity is material for a picture — or a whole series of pictures, showing the operation step by step. Plowing, seeding, cultivating, harvesting, threshing, feeding, milking — each of these has dozens of pictorial moments. Farm equipment against a skyline offers picturesque foreground material for sunset shots. The orchard in bloom is a hunting-ground for blossom close-ups — and a pleasant setting for pictures of people, too. And there are dozens of nooks and corners to yield unexpected still-life material for your photographic sketch book.

farm animals—better than a zoo

When you want to take animal pictures, and are far from a zoo — just go to the nearest farm. Pictorially, a cow is as good material as a camel — and sometimes better. A mare with her foal, a hen with her brood of chicks, a flock of ducks, a handsome   117

turkey gobbler anxiously awaiting Thanksgiving — there's no better picture material anywhere. Whether you're after serious pictorial studies, or shots with a touch of humor, you'll find ample opportunity here.

Be sure, however, to have your Kodak Portra Lens at hand. Some of the subjects — such as chicks or ducklings — are very small. For satisfying results, they must be pictured at close range, and a Portra Lens enables you to do just that.

pictures in the winter, too

Winter in the country, especially in areas of heavy snow, is as fruitful pictorially as the spring or summer. Shadows on the snow, ski trails or rabbit tracks, farm chores, brooks frozen over or breaking open in the January thaw, winter landscapes — all these are material for the camera, and almost every summer opportunity has a pictorial winter counterpart. There's plenty of color in the winter scene, too. Evergreens, red barns, blue snow shadows under a blue sky, and the rich hues of winter sunsets, all offer invitation to the camera and Kodak color film.

That's one of photography's many fine features. It isn't tied to any one spot on the calendar. Every season is a picture season.

Pictures from the air

IF YOU FLY, take your camera along. Excellent pictures can be taken from the air with amateur cameras — although, of course, the amateur camera with a fast lens and fast shutter enjoys a definite advantage.

You'll find worth-while pictorial material wherever you are. Cities, rivers, mountains, towering cloud formations, farmsteads amid a varied pattern of tilled fields, dams, and harbors — all merit your camera's attention. Commercial airlines are happy to have you bring your camera, and their hostesses can generally help you with advice on photographic technique. If you fly in a private plane, you may maneuver for low-altitude close-ups of notable features and landmarks, in your own community and elsewhere.

basic technique is simple

There are just a few simple, basic points to remember. Don't let your camera touch any part of the plane, or vibration will blur the picture. Select a shutter speed adequate for the altitude and ground speed (see table, Page 120). Use a filter to cut through atmospheric haze. And in an open plane, surround the camera bellows with a metal shield firmly braced to the camera body and lens support, so the slip-stream won't collapse it.

Under ideal conditions and at relatively high altitudes, acceptable aerial pictures have been taken with simple-lens cameras; but it is safer and better to equip yourself at the start with a camera that has a good fast lens and a high-speed shutter.

either color or black-and-white

For black-and-white shots, choose a panchromatic or infrared film. Kodak Plus-X Film, fast and fine-grained, is an ideal choice; it will yield superior enlargements (and to be viewed properly, any aerial view should be enlarged at least to 8x10 inches). For dramatic long-range views, Kodak Infrared Film with a Kodak Wratten A Filter is an excellent combination.

Any of the Kodak full-color films is suitable for aerial work (Kodachrome Roll Film for miniature-camera shots; Kodak Ektachrome Film or Kodachrome Professional Sheet Film for press-type and similar cameras; and Kodacolor Film or Kodak Ektachrome Roll Film for popular-size roll-film cameras).

these are basic shutter speeds

In the air, your shutter speed is determined by the speed of the plane and its altitude. For instance, at 100 miles per hour and 1,000 feet altitude, the minimum safe shutter speed is 1/200 second. This table shows the minimums for other speeds and altitudes:

ALTITUDE (in feet)	GROUND SPEED IN MILES PER HOUR				
	75	100	125	150	200
4000 and up	1/50	1/50	1/50	1/50	1/100
3000 to 4000	1/50	1/50	1/100	1/100	1/100
2000 to 3000	1/100	1/100	1/100	1/100	1/200
1000 to 2000	1/200	1/200	1/200	1/400	1/400
500 to 1000	1/400	1/400	1/400	1/800	1/800

Best practice, of course, is to use a still higher shutter speed — if your lens speed permits. Depth of field is not a problem; in aerial work you set the focus at infinity, and leave it there.

The effect of the plane's speed is minimized in "oblique" views, with the camera pointed ahead of the plane or to the rear, rather than straight down or straight out the side.

This aerial view illustrates a number of points — including one way to put a foreground into an aerial photograph! It was taken on Kodachrome Film, while a cloud shadow lay on the city, providing a cool, subdued background for the warm-toned, sunlit seaplane. For the city to dominate, of course, it should be crisply sunlit — with front light or side light for color, or side light for black-and-white. Bear this in mind when you choose the hour to go up, if you want to picture a particular location from a particular direction. In this picture, the cloud shadow produces an effect similar to that of ground haze, which is often present; to subdue the bluish effect, take along a Kodak Skylight Filter for color shots, or, for black-and-white shots on panchromatic film, a Wratten G Filter. For dramatic contrasts in black-and-white aerial views, the proper filter is the Wratten A (red), with panchromatic or infrared film.

121

follow this exposure guide

Determine the correct shutter speed from the preceding table; then arrive at the lens opening by conversion of the values shown below. For example 1/100 at *f*/8 is the equivalent of 1/200 at *f*/5.6 or 1/400 at *f*/4. Your Snapshot Kodaguide is a handy device for making the conversion; it shows the equivalents at any setting.

SCENES IN BRIGHT SUN	Kodachrome Daylight Type 35mm., Bantam	Kodak Ekta-chrome or Sheet Koda-chrome	Kodacolor	Plus-X	Infrared with Kodak Wratten A Filter
Average scenes with houses, trees, fields	1/100, f/4.5	1/50, f/4.5	1/100, f/5.6	1/100, f/8*	1/100 between f/5.6-f/8
Bright scenes, deserts, beaches.	1/100, f/5.6	1/50, f/5.6	1/100, f/6.3	1/100 between f/8-f/11†	1/100 between f/5.6-f/8

*Plus-X with Wratten G (haze-cutting) filter, 1/100, f/4.5   †Plus-X with G filter, 1/100 f/5.6

With color films balanced for daylight, a Kodak Skylight Filter can be used to reduce the effect of bluish ground haze. No increase in exposure is required. Kodachrome or Kodacolor Film, Type A, can be used in aerial shots with the Type A Filter For Daylight; no other filter is needed.

122

This aerial view of a river gorge is typical of the pictorial material you are likely to find in almost any locality. Obviously, it's a picture that could be obtained only from the air; from no other position could the full-circle reflection of the bridge, and the surrounding area, be captured. You need no special equipment to obtain such shots; this picture was taken with a regular hand camera, on Kodak Plus-X Film. For least motion, in such a shot, the plane should be approaching or leaving the subject; with the plane flying parallel to the subject, a higher shutter speed is required.

Vacations, holidays, and family events

THERE'S JUST ONE best way to picture a vacation, or any other holiday or family event. Start at the beginning, and make a picture story that carries through right to the end.

A good picture story of a vacation begins long before the vacation does. Take the first pictures when you begin planning the holiday. Picture Dad as he fondly polishes his fishing tackle, Mother flourishing a new bathing suit and arguing for the lake or the seashore, and the baby happily chewing up a travel folder. When you begin packing, spare a moment to picture that, too; there are always entertaining situations. Start another chapter when you load up and take off, and so on, right through.

don't rely on sound effects

A picture which has to be explained is *not* a good story-picture. Try to make each one so clear and definite that it tells its own story — at a glance. This calls for a little more effort (until you get the knack of it) but it's well worth while.

En route, check off the important or interesting spots you'll visit, and plan your "picture coverage" for each one. Not necessarily specific shots, but certainly the general story you want to tell. If, for example, you're visiting Mount Vernon, you'll want a pictorial story of how George Washington lived. Pursuing that theme when you arrive, you'll certainly take pictures of the view over the Potomac from his veranda, the garden with its espaliered fruit trees and formal vegetable beds, the coach house,

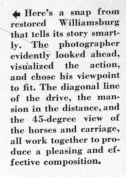

Here's a snap from restored Williamsburg that tells its story smartly. The photographer evidently looked ahead, visualized the action, and chose his viewpoint to fit. The diagonal line of the drive, the mansion in the distance, and the 45-degree view of the horses and carriage, all work together to produce a pleasing and effective composition.

Full color is definitely in order for vacations and travel — whether you're fishing among southern cypresses or touring in Grand Canyon country (facing page). In the fishing scene, the delicate coloring of the water, emphasized by the sharp red accent of the canoe, retains all its realism in color. In the canyon view, the warm foreground, the blue middle ground, and the misty aqua of the far ridges and pinnacles, provide depth and atmospheric separation. ➡

Color films are not as fast as most black-and-white films — but on sunny days, with an f/4.5 or faster lens, you can easily picture fairly fast action that's not too close to the camera. In this shot, note how the photographer's figure at right helps direct your eye to the dramatic rodeo action in midfield. The far hill also helps "frame" the action — so it's fully as effective as it would be nearer to the camera.

close-ups of the signal bell and various novel architectural details — and anything else that helps convey the atmosphere and character of the place.

don't shoot at random

Remember that each picture has a job to do. It must tell part of the story for you. Select your subject matter, viewpoint, and camera distance with care. Economize on film by making each shot count.

Warn members of your family not to look at the camera. It's easy enough to take "see the birdie" pictures at home. Get your folks to show interest in the things you're picturing. When you photograph a landscape, put them in the foreground — admiring the view, not you. When you record a historical plaque or explanatory road sign, show them reading the sign or taking notes from it. (Incidentally, snaps of such signs are highly desirable; they help knit the vacation story together.)

126

Every picture on these two pages has a story to tell — and tells it clearly, directly, without waste of time. This could be part of the record of your own vacation in the country. Note how simple each shot is—how it includes only what is needed for the story, with everything else ruled out.

but don't omit people

Whenever possible, include one or more members of the family in the picture. This personalizes the record, and makes it definitely yours. But always remember to show people doing something that's part of the vacation, and *not* stiffly posed for the camera.

Items of exceptional interest generally deserve more than one picture. Get a general shot from the best viewpoint; then move in for close-ups of significant details.

Final step in the vacation narrative is to arrange all the pictures, in sequence, with a note regarding date and place, in a special vacation album. Add a new chapter each year, and in a few seasons you'll have a book of memories that's beyond price.

stories of other holidays

The year is studded with other holidays and events that demand a pictorial story. Christmas, of course, leads the list. Well in

Study each of these pictures, and the simple devices that focus your attention on the "story." Every person pictured is looking at the object of main concern — the axe blade, the lamb, the ear of corn — so, you look too. Most of the backgrounds are simple, with no distracting detail. And all the action is clear — understandable at a glance.

Christmas pictured in color is Christmas at its best. Picture it all — putting major emphasis on close-ups, the tree and its colorful decorations, bright new toys as they're put into action. Provide plenty of light for the indoor snaps — and use your Snapshot Kodaguide or Flash Kodaguide to get the exposures exactly right.

advance, make a list of things to be covered: gift buying, the wrapping of gifts, mailing and personal delivery (by all means let the children do the actual delivering), decorating the tree, hanging the stockings (check back to Page 80 for a helpful note on fireplace shots), the gifts arrayed under the tree, the children asleep Christmas night (if they can actually get to sleep), the miracle of discovery in the morning (and the expressions on their

Be sure to take a time exposure of the outdoor decorations. This is a 15-second exposure at $f/11$ on Kodachrome Film, Type A. A flash lamp was set off to give some general illumination (but not too much) on the house front and snow.

Start the Christmas story ahead of time — when the children first begin thinking about that wonderful man (above). When you go shopping, take your camera along — and you may bring home a masterpiece such as the snap of the enraptured young miss at right. It's a great picture!

faces), opening the wrapped gifts (with more expressions and excitement), first tryouts of the new train or bike or sled or skates, at least one shot of the general clutter of gifts and wrappings, Christmas-dinner shots of the family and the carving of the turkey, a close-up showing the breaking of the wishbone — and maybe even shots of someone catching an after-dinner nap.

With such a scenario, planned ahead, you can be sure of a story that's satisfyingly complete — without blank spots you'd always regret.

130

On Christmas ➡ Day, as you take other snaps, try some like this. Then you'll be all set for next year's photographic Christmas greeting cards. Don't just copy this idea — improve on it so that it's new and all yours.

⬅ In a snapshot, this joyous grin will last long after the new car is worn out.

thanksgiving, halloween, easter

Thanksgiving usually provides material for family group pictures; Halloween furnishes a whole sequence — selection of the pumpkin, carving the jack-o'-lantern, lighting it up, trying on the false faces and costumes, the party activities with fortune-telling and bobbing for apples and all the rest. Easter, like any other dress-up occasion, has a costume story to be told — including the selection and home trials of the new ensembles, as well as their first public appearance.

birthday parties belong in the album

Every child's birthday is a milestone to be remembered — and each birthday dinner or special children's party deserves a series of pictures. The technique is the same — start at the beginning, or earlier, and follow right through to the end. Picture the child greeting his guests; show the acceptance of the gifts, and the un-

131

Always show activity — "something doing" — and your party snaps will really tell the story.

← Color tells the story with extra realism — keeps it right down to the last detail. These bright Easter eggs are, of course, an obvious subject for color. But color film is not limited to such occasions — it adds an extra touch to pictures of almost any family event.

← Like Christmas, Halloween offers special opportunity for a color story. In activity pictures, such as the three on this page, keep reasonably close to your subjects — and limit the picture to just those elements that "tell the story." Excess background should be eliminated at top, bottom, and sides, so it doesn't compete with the important material.

← Any new pet is material for a biography in full color. And the biography of the pet's master can be recounted in color too. Note how the simple backgrounds aid these three pictures — in each one, the action stands out clearly, so you grasp the situation at a glance. If a picture needs to be explained, it isn't a good story-picture.

Color film is important in telling the wedding story — even when most of the colors are delicate pastels. Always bear that in mind, when you're using color film. It's not necessary to have big, splashy areas of brilliant "saturated" color — such as royal blue, fire-engine red, emerald green, and flaming orange. In fact, too much intense color will give you "color indigestion." Soft, harmonious colors tend to produce pictures that are more pleasing — and that you enjoy seeing for a longer time.

133

wrapping; snap high moments in the games; capture a shot of the cake as it's brought in, and another as the candles are blown out. You may think you're being prodigal with film; but in years to come, whenever you review the pictures, you'll be sorry you didn't take twice as many.

Be careful, in picturing all these special events, not to confine yourself to general views. Mix in a generous seasoning of short-range shots and close-ups. Those are the pictures that really carry the story along.

anniversaries—very important

Every anniversary calls for a shot or two of the celebrants and their anniversary gifts. If it's an extra-special anniversary, it demands a trip to your portrait photographer, for a formal portrait you'll distribute to relatives and friends. But there are always additional snapshots to be taken at home, for your own private and personal albums.

134

◄ What constitutes a "family event," anyway? Thanksgiving dinner is obviously one — and Grandfather's ceremonious operation on the turkey is certainly a picture for the record. Just as surely, Junior's hopeful, premature search for the first whisker belongs in your family's picture history. ↓

Picturing
children and pets

WHEN YOU TAKE PICTURES of your child — make it a pleasant experience for the child. Don't overwork your model; don't insist on taking pictures if a child wants to do something else.

Almost any child is a willing model, if his or her interest is first aroused. Instead of asking the child to pose, suggest taking a picture of something else — a pet, a favorite doll, or some other toy. Then ask the child to *help* you get the picture; let Johnny put the dog through his tricks, or let Sue feed her dolls or tuck them into bed. This indirect approach not only helps eliminate self-consciousness; it also provides action and a story theme for the pictures. Often the youngster will be more interested in the camera than in anything else. Very well, let him handle it, look   135

"Help me take a picture of the rabbit eating a carrot." — "Help me take a picture of your dolls." It's a grand way to put the child at ease for pictures.

through the finder and take a snap himself. Then, usually, he'll be willing for you to take over.

by all means, be casual

Picture taking should be a normal, more or less everyday experience; as simple and casual as the child's bath or afternoon nap. Don't make it seem special; don't create a furore just because you have a camera in your hands. Make the child your picture-taking partner as well as your model. Let him suggest things to take; his picture ideas will generally deal with things in his own small world, which is precisely what you want. As early as possible, teach him how to operate a simple camera.

Try not to waste film on stiffly posed, doing-nothing, "see-the-birdie" pictures. The heart-warming snapshots are those which show child activity — playing with toys and pets, bathing, eating,

← Color is the natural medium for pictures of children — either Kodachrome or Kodacolor Film. Choose simple action, a simple setting, harmonious colors, and close viewpoint. Reflections from wall soften the lighting in this shot.

Bathroom walls help you get soft light, too — and the bath provides action to be pictured. Here, incidentally, is one location where your small, lively subject is likely to "stay put." ➡

← Child, pet, and action—they make a perfect combination for human-interest pictures. Note the good grouping in this one, and the simplicity—nothing to confuse the story idea.

137

A novel detail, or a treatment that's "just a little different," often yields outstanding pictures. The snapshot above is a perfect example. And any new toy may serve as a "springboard" for a series of good pictures revealing the child's pleasure and excitement. ➡

blowing bubbles, sniffing flowers, helping with housework, reading picture books, building snow men, trying out a new tricycle, playing marbles, making a model airplane, learning to sew, wading, swimming, playing with the lawn hose, and so on. Focus on those themes, and you're on your way to a rich and satisfying picture story of the child's early years.

some are natural actors, some are not

Properly accustomed to picture taking, most children can "make believe" successfully for the camera. Try both the "let's make believe" and the "help me take this" method, and concentrate on the one that works best with your child.

But don't fool around. Know what you want in the picture, and snap it promptly. If you fumble along, seeking perfect lighting and perfect posing, the child will tire and lose interest. Shoot one picture, so he can see progress; then renew his interest by suggesting another shot, just a bit different.

139

◄ Maybe this delightfully humorous picture is a bit of "make believe" – if so, the young subject has a future as an actor. Many children quickly grasp the spirit of a picture idea, and can act a simple part with surprising aplomb. Try it with your own child.

with pets—a natural combination

Play between child and pet always yields pictures. There's no better combination anywhere. If you photograph a pet by himself, provide a toy or activity for him — a bowl of milk or ball of string for the kitten, a bone or ball for the pup. Often, this will help make your subject "stay put," so you can take accurate close-ups with a Kodak Portra Lens over your camera lens.

For most snaps of children or pets, bring your camera down lower than usual—to the subject's own eye level. This often gives the child a keener sense of participation, and often shows pets to better advantage. Some scenes, of course — such as a game of marbles, or a table at a children's party — are much better from a high viewpoint, aiming down.

continuity: "sequence" pictures

Every picture you take of your child is part of a long biography — the child's growing-up story. Tell this story properly, and by the time Betty or Junior turns twelve, you will have filled many a fat album.

Some chapters and details in this story cannot be told in a single picture. A snapshot sequence, such as that below, is needed . . . three or four or a dozen pictures that trace the action or event step by step. Only by making a sequence can you show the child's whole reaction, or show the story building up to a climax. It calls for fast, sure operation of your camera — but a good picture sequence is worth every bit of effort you expend.

Not every story can be told in one picture — sometimes a series is essential. When the activity lasts long enough, take several pictures; then arrange the prints in your album in the best "story sequence." Keep the camera viewpoint and distance about the same for all the shots, as in the simple three-picture sequence shown here. ➡

140

↑ For small subjects, rely on your close-up lens (a Kodak Portra Lens or Kodak Close-up Attachment). These slip-on lenses work with any camera.

Activities of pets also → yield "story" pictures. Just observe the facial expression of this ingenious kitten. Obviously, it's a gay, warm, wonderful world he's found — and it makes a marvelous human-interest picture.

"series" opportunities are many

In addition to short, quick sequences — several pictures covering an event that may take only a few moments — there are many opportunities for a leisurely series of pictures, all related to each   141

here's a day in the life of a busy young woman

make a series like this for your own album

1. Good morning!

2. Let's get this over fast.

3. Suppose it's got to be done.

6. You teeter—I'll totter.

7. Not a bad story.

other by some common theme. A picture story of the child's typical day — rising, dressing, breakfast, play in the yard, helping Mother, reading a story, playing indoors with toys, supper, the bath, going to bed — is an excellent example. Make one such series at a strategic time each year. Special occasions, such as a birthday, offer "series" material; include one picture, each birth-

4. All right, Tuffy—let's go!

5. Watch me "pump."

Makes me feel like a new woman.

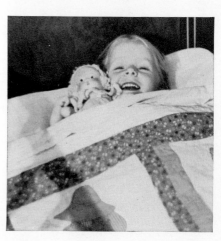

9. Good night!

day, of the child with Mother or Father, for a record of year-by-year growth.

Make "series" records, too, as new interests or activities develop — a picture story of preparations for the first day of school, the fitting and wearing of the first party dress, a day at Junior's first summer camp when you visit him, his progress in his first hobby, the complete welcome given to a new pet. Each new

Every picture in this group could be developed into a worth-while series — with various steps in primping at the left, progress of the gossip session at lower left, stages in the kitten's inquiries, variations in Johnny's face as he reviews the Sunday comics.

Child close-ups in color have ➡ great appeal — and enlarged prints make wonderful gifts for friends and fond relatives. While a behind-the-camera lighting is common for color, unusually charming effects can be obtained with back lighting, as here. The sun is slightly to the rear, illuminating only one side of the forehead and cheek; the rest of the face is illuminated by a reflector (such as a white sheet, newspaper, or white wall). This avoids squinting, and helps keep delicate flesh tones. For an extreme close-up, such as this, a camera with long-focus lens is best; for example, a Kodak Tourist Camera fitted with a miniature adapter kit for color film. Incidentally, the warmth of flesh tones in a back-lighted shot is affected by the color of the reflector. A warm-tinted reflector yields very warm flesh tones, as here; light from a blue sky produces cooler tones.

⬅ Here is another departure from ordinary "flat front lighting." The subject was seated close to a window; reflections from the book in his lap, and from other nearby objects, illuminated the shadow side of his face. Without such shadow illumination, the effect would tend to be harsh; with it, a charming effect, akin to the lighting in certain Dutch and Flemish portraits, has been achieved. Exposure for such shots will vary with the size of the window and brightness of the day; this was on Kodachrome Film, Daylight Type, about ½ second at f/4.5.

145

sport a child undertakes can be made the basis of a picture series: learning to use the first sled or ride the first bike, learning to skate, learning to play football or baseball, learning to ride a horse or pony. In short, almost any child activity offers you a snapshot story — and they all belong in your permanent picture collection.

Family singing, and other musical activities, offer wide opportunity for story sequences — serious or humorous, special-occasion or everyday. ➡

⬆ School activities are also rich in picture opportunity — and the record of those irreplaceable days must be made now or never. Time won't wait — except in snapshots.

Picturing people

WHEN YOU PICTURE A PERSON, you want a natural, truthful rendering — a "speaking likeness." You want your subject to appear exactly *as you know him.*

So, forget about formal portraits. Leave them to the studio photographer — who has special camera equipment for such work, and special training in using it. Devote your efforts to informal portraiture — your subject in his natural environment, his natural activities — for which your *amateur* camera is better fitted than a big studio camera.

If your subject is a fishing enthusiast, picture him in fishing dress — or at his home workbench, tying flies. If he is a great

147

Picture folks as you know them—and in their natural surroundings—not all stiff, starched, and "prettied up" for the camera.

⬆ Make full use of color film — and pictures of people will be just that much more real. What could be more natural, unaffected, "true to life," than this friendly study of a family doctor at his office desk?

Color studies of people can be made almost anywhere outdoors — but highly reflective surroundings, such as beaches, snow slopes, bright tennis courts, and open water, have special advantages.

⬅ In this shot, observe how reflections from the sand illuminate the shadows, keeping them soft and retaining delicate color.

For most pictures of people, a conventional lighting is used — one light near the camera, another to the side of the subject and placed somewhat above the level of the subject's head. But for special purposes, other arrangements of lighting can be used.

At right, the main ➜ light has been placed low, and aimed up — something that always gives a theatrical or "footlight" effect. Here, it's suitable. The best way to learn lighting is simply to experiment with various arrangements — and observe what happens.

reader, show him with a favorite book, in a favorite chair. If he smokes a pipe, let him enjoy it in your pictures. Include the *hands* in your pictures; they're often as expressive as the face.

simple, basic lighting is best

Good portraiture is largely a matter of good lighting — once you have placed your subject in his natural setting, and achieved a natural, "un-self-conscious" pose. Simple lighting is almost always preferable; outdoors, sunshine plus a reflector, and indoors, two photo lights, or one light and a reflector.

"Reflector" here merely means anything that will reflect light to your subject — a white sheet, a newspaper, a light-colored room wall indoors, or a light-colored house wall outdoors. A magazine in a subject's lap, outdoors or under a reading lamp, will act as a reflector, softening the shadows of the face and improving the gradation of tones.

149

← This is a conventional lighting — the one you will find most useful. One light to the right, fairly close to the subject; a second light close to the camera, to "fill in" the shadows, making them soft and bright. Seek a pleasant balance of illumination between the shadow areas and the "highlight" areas — not too strong a contrast, not too weak.

For sculptural effect, the best "beginning" combination is a strong light to one side, and a secondary light toward the front (see the diagram above). For each subject, the positions are altered by trial and error, until a placement is found which best reveals the form of the person's features. This simple basic lighting also applies to other subjects and situations — whenever you want to reveal the shape of solid forms.

keep the backgrounds simple

A spotty or "scrambled" background, filled with extraneous and irrelevant objects or patches, will spoil the portrait. Select your viewpoint so that a plain background comes behind the subject

— or place your subject before a plain background. If you can't do either, try to contrive your lighting so that the background is in *shadow*.

Window draperies or curtains — assuming they are not conspicuously figured — often make pleasant backgrounds for indoor daytime pictures. Place your subject beside the window, so that daylight illuminates one side of the face; and place a reflector or lamp so that the shadow side of the face is softly illuminated. On Kodak Verichrome or Kodak Plus-X Film, on a sunny day with the subject not more than three feet from the window and out of direct sun, make your trial exposure 1/5 to 1/10 second at *f*/6.3 (or 2 to 6 seconds if you're using a simple-lens camera).

synchronized flash for candor

For casual portraits of people doing things, synchronized flash is ideal. A single flash lamp, mounted on the camera, does not

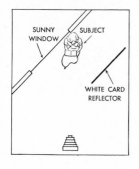

A window makes a pleasing setting for pictures of people. Use a reflector (or photoflood lamp) on the shadow side, as in the diagram, to balance the shadow illumination. Subject here is in direct sun; 1/25, *f*/8. ➡

151

yield the sculptural "modeling" you can obtain from two or more flood lamps; but the flash *does* allow you to capture many a moment which would be lost if you took time to arrange flood lights.

odd angles — their risks and uses

The normal camera level is the subject's own eye-level — a bit higher sometimes if he has a too-prominent chin, or a bit lower if his forehead is too prominent. However, a very low position can sometimes be used outdoors if you want the sky for a pleasing plain background. A very high position may be used for a picture that's interesting and different, worth while because of its novelty of presentation.

Informal family portraiture should be one of your camera's chief uses—because each portrait is a contribution to the family's pictorial history, an important project for any hobbyist's camera.

152

In picturing people, try things that are interesting and different. That's the way to learn. Some experiments will turn out happily — others will teach you what NOT to do. At left, the unusually high viewpoint and dark masses of tone help create a definite "mood" for the picture. Below, a low viewpoint brings in an interesting sky background, and the net is neatly employed to complete the setting. Keep your work informal. Don't try to imitate "formal" studio portraits; the professional can do those much better than you can.

Pictures
after dark

TIME WAS when cameras went to bed at sundown. Now—thanks to modern film and modern cameras — the snapshot day extends right around the clock. Wherever you have light, even if it's only moonlight or candlelight, you can take pictures.

For most after-dark pictures, there are two favorite light sources — the midget photoflash lamp, and the photoflood lamp. The photoflood lamps are used indoors, on regular house current, and there are several types (pictured on Page 154). The midget flash lamps are used with small flashlight batteries, indoors or out, as shown on Page 155.

lamp-to-subject distance is important

If you're reading this book by artificial light, bring it up close to the light and observe the brightness of the page. Now, move it several feet farther away, and observe how the brightness diminishes.

That illustrates the most important point in all picture taking by artificial light. The farther your photo lamp is from your subject, the less light your subject receives. To make up for any increase in distance, you must increase the time of exposure — *or*, you must use a wider lens opening. Otherwise, the picture will be underexposed.

On Page 160 is a table which gives correct exposure for the most popular Kodak films at various lamp-to-subject distances. Follow this table, and your flash and flood shots will be correctly

these are the tools for pictures after dark..

Photoflood lamps (at left) are basic lighting at home, when the situation permits arranging two or more lights for a desired effect. (For "spur-of-the-moment" shots, use flash, shown below.) The small No. 1 photoflood is equivalent, in photographically effective brilliance, to about fifteen 50-watt lamps; the larger No. 2 is twice as bright and lasts twice as long. Either one will serve for many snapshot sessions. Use them in a Kodak Vari-Beam Standlight (at right), or in a Kodak Vari-Beam Clamplight.

Reflector Photoflood lamps (at left) have the same brightness as a No. 2 photoflood in an efficient metal reflector. They can be used in any house socket or lamp; adjustable bridge lamps are handy. All photofloods get very hot, so don't let them touch draperies, lamp shades, or your hands.

Ordinary house lamps (at left) are not very bright compared to photoflood lamps; but they can be used for time exposures. Use a "Home Lighting" Kodaguide for exposure guidance.

Midget flash lamps (at left) are only about as big as a walnut; but they pack a powerful punch. Each lamp yields one picture. You use them in a Kodak Photo Flasher (at left), a Kodak Flasholder (below, right), or a flash synchronizer. These lamps can also be used outdoors, with Flasholder or synchronizer, to illuminate deep shadows.

Kodak Photo Flasher (at left) is inexpensive unit for "open flash" shots (described on next page). Slip a flash lamp into the socket, press the button, and the lamp flashes.

Kodak Flasholder (at right) is a moderately-priced accessory for Kodak cameras with flash shutters. The lamp is set off at the right moment as you trip the shutter.

These pocket guides (Flash Kodaguide, Snapshot Kodaguide, and Home Lighting Kodaguide) assure success in pictures "after dark."

FLASH Indoors at night, you can make "open flash" snaps with any camera that sets for "T" or "B." Set the shutter on "T" or "B," and put the camera on a firm support, aimed at the subject. Put a flash lamp in a Kodak Photo Flasher; aim it at the subject; open the camera shutter; flash the lamp; close the shutter.

A Kodak Flasholder or synchronizer mounted on the camera makes it easier — enables you to move about freely, and shoot when you're ready. You trip the camera shutter; the shutter flashes the lamp. Correct distances and lens openings for various films and the popular midget lamps are all tabulated on Page 160.

With a Kodak Flasholder or synchronizer, you can also use flash outdoors in deep shade and in back-lighted shots, to assure better shadow detail. It is best to find out by experiment just how much shadow brilliance you prefer; start out with Kodak Verichrome Film, $f/16$, 1/25 second, and a No. 5 lamp ten feet from the subject, or an SM lamp at seven feet. If this makes the shadows too bright for your taste, increase the distance or stretch a handkerchief over the flash reflector in later shots. For outdoor flash after dark, see top of Page 162.

No. 1—3½ ft.   No. 2—3½ ft.

FLOOD At right is a basic setup for simple cameras, or other cameras set at 1/25 and $f/11$, with Kodak Super-XX Film and a No. 1 and a No. 2 photoflood lamp in reflector units. Note that the No. 2 (the stronger or "key" light) is placed well to the side of the subject, while the No. 1 is more to the front, as near as possible to the "axis" line between subject and camera. This arrangement yields an "unsymmetrical" distribution of light, which helps bring out the form of the subject.

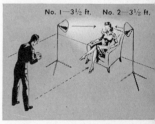

This is a more elaborate arrangement, with an extra light at floor level to illuminate the background and subdue shadows cast by the subject. For color shots, the two major lights should be of about the same intensity, so that shadows are barely strong enough to see; otherwise, picture contrast tends to appear harsh. A photoelectric exposure meter, if correctly used, is helpful when more than the two basic lights are used, or when light-to-subject distances are altered.

Here, a reflector is being used in place of a side light, and a "back-light" has been placed high and to the rear of the subjects, to illuminate their hair. Exposure is based on the main light, facing the subjects. Many interesting and unusual effects can be evolved with only a few lights. Do not use more than six No. 1 lamps, or three No. 2 lamps, on one 15-ampere house circuit. Turn lamps off when not in use.

155

up photo lights here — but
sh assured a good picture.

Flash gets the credit, too, for this
pleasing, wholly natural study. ➤

exposed. More convenient still, equip yourself with an inexpensive Kodaguide, one of the types pictured on Page 154.

flash with one photoflash lamp

Most photoflash shots are taken with a single lamp, in a holder mounted on the camera. Modern Kodak cameras are built with electrical contacts in the shutter, so that the lamp flashes at the moment the shutter is opened. Many other cameras which have setting-type shutters can be fitted with a "synchronizer" which produces the same result. All you do is put a flash lamp in the socket, stand back at the desired distance from your subject, set the lens at the correct opening (Page 160), and take a snapshot— just as if you were outdoors in broad daylight.

Each flash lamp flashes just once. One or more lamps can be used on extensions for special pictorial effects, just as photoflood lamps are placed for special effects (see below).

With a camera which does not have built-in flash contacts or a cable-release socket, *but can be set for "time" or "bulb" exposures,* you simply use a Kodak Photo Flasher. Set the camera for "T" or "B," place it on a firm support, aim the Photo Flasher at your subject, then open the shutter, flash the lamp in the Photo Flasher, and close the shutter. You can hold the Photo Flasher high or low, left or right, for special effects.

flood, with two or more lamps

An advantage of photoflood lamps is that several can be used as easily as one — which enables you to work out interesting and pictorially effective lighting arrangements. However, don't use more than three Reflector Photofloods, or three No. 2 photofloods, or six No. 1 photofloods, on a 15-ampere house circuit. If more lamps are used, plug them into different circuits.

No. 1 and No. 2 photoflood lamps should always be used in efficient metal reflectors. For the No. 2 lamps, the Kodak Vari-Beam Standlight and Clamplight are ideal reflector units. The

Every change made in the position of a photo light produces changes in the picture effect. Down low, near floor level and shining up, a theatrical or firelight effect ensues, as at left. At right, the lights have been placed for a pleasing natural effect, to bring out the details of the uniform and the shape of the subject's features. Do a lot of experimenting with light positions — you'll make some errors, but it's the only way to learn. Watch out for the distance from lights to subject; that determines what exposure is correct. (See Page 160.)

FLASH EXPOSURES

with a Kodak Photo Flasher (or Kodak Flasholder on a Kodak camera with flash shutter set at 1/25 second).

FLASH LAMP	KODAK FILM	GUIDE NO.*	DISTANCE, LAMP TO SUBJECT, IN FEET, INDOORS					
			5	7	10	14	20	30
ONE NO. 5 OR 25 LAMP ***	SUPER-XX	200	f/32-45	f/22-32	f/16-22	f/16-11	f/11-8	f/6.3
	VERICHROME	110	f/22	f/16	f/11	f/8	f/5.6	f/3.5
	PLUS-X	140	f/22-32	f/16-22	f/11-16	f/8-11	f/5.6-8	f/4.5
	KODACHROME TYPE A**	70	f/16	f/11	f/8	f/5.6	FOR AVERAGE SUBJECTS	
		60 ➡	f/16 11	f/11-8	f/6.3	f/4.5	⬅ FOR DARK SUBJECTS	
	KODACOLOR TYPE A**	95	f/16-22	f/11-16	f/8-11	f/5.6-8	FOR AVERAGE SUBJECTS	
		80 ➡	f/16	f/11	f/8	f/5.6	⬅ FOR DARK SUBJECTS	
ONE "SM" OR "SF" LAMP ***	SUPER-XX	110	f/22	f/16	f/11	f/8	f/5.6	f/3.5-4.5
	VERICHROME	60	f/11-16	f/8-11	f/6.3	f/4.5	f/2.8-4	f/2
	PLUS-X	75	f/16	f/11	f/8	f/5.6	f/4	f/2.8
	KODACHROME TYPE A**	45	f/8-11	f/6.3	f/4.5	f/2.8-4	FOR AVERAGE SUBJECTS	
		40 ➡	f/8	f/5.6	f/4	f/2.8	⬅ FOR DARK SUBJECTS	
	KODACOLOR TYPE A**	50	f/11	f/8	f/5.6	f/4	FOR AVERAGE SUBJECTS	
		45 ➡	f/8-11	f/6.3	f/4.5	f/2.8-4	⬅ FOR DARK SUBJECTS	

*Guide numbers are a quick, handy means of finding correct exposure. Simply divide the NUMBER into the DISTANCE from lamp to subject—and you get the correct LENS OPENING. Example: Guide Number 75 ÷ 5 feet = f/15 (very close to f/16). Where two f/numbers are shown above (such as f/11-8) set the lens index between them. The numbers in this table are guides for average cameras; you should adjust them up or down to fit the performance of your particular lens and shutter. **For best full-color rendering on these color films, use no filter with SM lamps; use a Kodak 81A Filter with SF lamps; a Kodak CC15 or 81C Filter with No. 5 lamps, and a Kodak 81D Filter with No. 25 lamps. ***Data for other film-and-lamp combinations are in the inexpensive, pocket-size FLASH KODAGUIDE, available from your Kodak dealer.

FLOOD

with two No. 2 Photoflood Lamps in Kodak Vari-Beam Standlights set at "still," or Kodaflectors (matte side). With color films, place *both* lamps at the distance marked * in each column below.

KODAK FILM	DISTANCE, EACH LAMP TO SUBJECT, IN FEET, INDOORS					
	3½* and 5	4* and 6	5* and 7	7* and 9	8* and 12	15* and 15*
SUPER-XX	1/25, f/11	1/25, f/8	1/25, f/6.3	1/25, f/5.6	1/25, f/4.5	1 sec, f/11
PLUS-X	1/25, f/8	1/25, f/5.6	1/25, f/4.5	1/25, f/4	1/10, f/5.6	2 sec, f/11
KODACHROME TYPE A**	1/25, f/4-4.5	1/25, f/4	1/10, f/5.6	1/10, f/4-4.5	1/5, f/5.6	4 sec, f/16
KODACOLOR TYPE A**	1/25, f/4.5	1/25, f/4.5	1/10, f/6.3	1/10, f/4.5	1/5, f/5.6	3 sec, f/16

For example: With Kodak Super-XX Film in the camera, one lamp 5 feet from the subject and one 7 feet, correct exposure is 1/25 second at f/6.3. With Kodachrome Film, Type A, both lamps 5 feet from subject, exposure is 1/10 second at f/5.6. At the "15-and-15" range, exposures are 1 or more full seconds; this is for views of room interiors. **Color exposures are for average subjects; for dark subjects, increase the lens opening one-half stop (for example, increase it from f/5.6 to between f/5.6 and 4) but keep the shutter speed and lamp distance the same. Exposure data for other shutter speeds, lamp distances, and lens openings are in the handy SNAPSHOT KODAGUIDE. Basic lighting arrangements are shown on Page 155.

Reflector Photofloods are, of course, a "sealed-beam" type of lamp, with the reflector built in.

A basic two-lamp plan is pictured on Page 155. It is correct either for snapshot exposures with simple cameras or other cameras set at 1/25 second and $f/11$ — the film in both cases is Kodak Super-XX Roll Film. Note that the two basic lights can be varied from left to right to suit the subject, but the lamp-to-subject distance must *not* be varied unless you adjust the lens opening or shutter speed to fit. Two *optional* "special-purpose" lights are also shown on Page 155 — one behind the subject to illuminate the background, and one overhead (shielded from the camera lens) to highlight the subject's hair. Learn the basic two-light arrangement, and you can then work out variations to suit special pictorial situations.

interiors — by flash or time exposure

Shots of whole room interiors or groups of people pose no special problems. You can take them by flash, flood, or regular room lighting. Just follow the table on Page 160 — but remember that during any exposure longer than 1/25 second, any people in the scene should hold still.

161

Various kinds of light can be mixed freely in black-and-white shots — but not for color films, except when you are seeking unusual or special effects. Here, if daylight comes from one side and photoflood light from the other, a picture on Kodachrome or Kodacolor Film, Type A, will tend to be very bluish in the daylit areas. That's wrong if you desire normal color rendering—but it may be just right if you want to suggest moonlight coming into the room window! ➡

outdoors after dark

When you go on a night outing — a picnic, a canoe ride, a swim, a night ski run, a horseback ride — take your flash camera along. You can get pictures anywhere. Use the "indoor" flash table on Page 160, basing your exposure on the distance from the flash lamp to a point *midway* between the nearest and farthest subjects of interest. For example, if the nearest person of a group is 10 feet from your flash lamp and the farthest person is 20 feet from the lamp, expose on the basis of 15 feet.

campfires — and other fires

Pictures of a campfire and campers can be taken by the light of the fire alone. Kodak Super-XX Film is the preferable film. Have the fire blazing brightly, group the party just close enough to be comfortable, and make a time exposure of 3 to 5 seconds at $f/8$ (or 6 to 10 seconds with a simple-lens camera).

For pictures of a burning building, outlined against a background of flames, expose 2 to 3 seconds at $f/8$ (4 to 6 seconds with a simple-lens camera) on Kodak Super-XX Film. Longer exposures will sometimes pick up detail in the surrounding scene. Too much exposure is better than not enough.

moonlight, street light, rain, snow, and fog

Scenic pictures can be taken by the light of a full moon; the exposures are long, but the results are well worth while. For a distant moonlit landscape, try 10 to 15 minutes at $f/8$ on Kodak Super-XX Film; for a nearby scene or landscape, double the exposure time.

Street lamps also permit interesting pictures. A time exposure of 30 seconds, at $f/8$, on Kodak Super-XX Film, will get almost any residential street scene; if the street is wet, 20 seconds will usually do; if it is covered with snow, 10 seconds. Brilliant business-section lighting permits still shorter exposures. Incidentally, people walking in front of the camera during a long time exposure are not likely to show, but the headlights of a passing automobile will record as long streaks of light. To pre-

Time exposures enable you to take pictures by street light and moonlight — wonderful pictures with interesting "mood" and delightful atmospheric quality. With modern Kodak films, it's easy! ➤

vent that, hold your hand in front of the lens until the automobile has gone by.

Rain, snow, and fog lend fascinating character to street scenes. When the night is misty, or snow is falling — that's when your camera should be up and doing. As soon as you *enjoy* going out on a nasty night to take pictures that can't be had at any other time, you're a true amateur photographer, one of the brotherhood.

floodlighted buildings are easy

Many public buildings, and fair or exposition structures, are floodlighted at night. With white floodlighting, an exposure of 30 to 60 seconds at $f/8$ on Kodak Super-XX Film will usually get the picture. On Kodachrome or Kodacolor Film, Type A, you can get *full-color* pictures of floodlighted buildings. It's best to use a large lens opening with the color film, and exposures of 4 to 15 seconds at $f/3.5$ (6 to 25 at $f/4.5$) will usually serve.

fireworks — black-and-white or color

Public fireworks spectacles at night yield dramatic pictures. Find a firm support on which to rest your camera, aim the camera at the sky where the bursts will occur, set it for "time" exposures, and open the shutter. After one burst has taken place within the field of the lens, you can close the shutter and wind the film — *or* you can leave it until several bursts have taken place, making a complicated tracery of light on the single film. With Kodak Super-XX Film, set the lens opening at $f/11$; for Kodachrome Film, Type A, use $f/5.6$ or $f/8$. To show spectators in the picture, for foreground interest, you can set off a flash during the time exposure.

theaters, and night sports events

These require a camera with a fast lens — at least $f/4.5$ for black-and-white shots on Kodak Super-XX Film, and $f/3.5$ or $f/2$ for full-color shots on Kodachrome Film, Type A. Scenes under brilliant spotlighting require exposures from 1/50 second at $f/4.5$

165

(for black-and-white) to 1/25 second at $f/2$ (for full color). Scenes under general illumination will require from 1/25 second at $f/4.5$ (for black-and-white) to 1/2 second at $f/2$ (for full color). Because of wide variations in lighting, it is desirable to keep an accurate record of exposures — and use the data as a guide when you revisit the same theater or arena for later pictures.

Sports and
action pictures

You don't have to go to the world series to take first-class sports pictures. Just look around your own neighborhood — to the nearest corner-lot baseball diamond, the high-school football field, the diving tower at your local swimming pool, the trotting races at the county fair, the tennis court in the next block, the nearest trout stream or boating water. The action is there, and who's to say that good snapshots of the neighborhood marble championship aren't as fine as any first-page sport shot that ever came out of Madison Square Garden?

And you don't need a super-de-luxe camera — although a fast lens and a fast shutter are real helps whenever you picture a

Winter and summer, wherever you are, there are sports picture opportunities. The pictures need not all be fast action; indeed, many moments and details that are rich in pictorial quality involve no fast motion at all. The ski shot at right is an example; just a bit of "atmosphere," but it would make an excellent cover for an album showing your child's first skiing adventures. The sports pictures that portray your own family and friends are the ones that count — in human interest and personal meaning.

subject in motion. Lacking these aids, you must put your reliance on ingenuity and accurate timing — and there will still be many an opportunity you must pass up.

fast motion that doesn't move

Study any sport, and you'll find moments when, for a fraction of a second, all motion is "frozen"— although the poses and attitudes of the players suggest violent action. The football player poised for a pass . . . the diver at the peak of his upward travel, before he starts down . . . the golfer at the precise end of his follow-through . . . you've seen 'em all.

Any camera can capture these action scenes — even the humblest box camera. All you need do is time your release accurately to catch the "poised moment." The fast shutter of a fine camera simply gives you a safety margin — it insures a sharp picture even if your timing judgment is a fraction off.

easy angles aid the simple camera

Watch an automobile as it comes down the street toward you. When a block away, it is approaching you "head-on," and hardly

169

◄ Who wants to take pictures of big-league baseball—when there are better pictures right around the corner? Here's a snap that has everything you want in a sports picture — expression, action, the sense of a thrilling moment. This is a "poised moment" (see text above); the actors are still and only the ball is in motion. With careful timing on your part, even a simple box camera can get such pictures. The motion in the ball is desirable; it accents the feeling of fast action.

Here's another "poised moment" — ball at the peak of the toss, racket back at the limit of its swing. Exposure was actually 1/500 second, but with careful timing by the photographer, a slower exposure would have served. Red filter was used, to darken the sky background. ➡

here's the secret of sharp action shots

The faster your subject moves in the view finder — the snappier your shutter speed must be. Movement depends on speed, distance, and angle.

One bike — but nine action situations. Close up, any subject calls for a faster shutter than when it's farther away. Coming or going, it doesn't move as fast in the finder as when it approaches at an angle or crosses straight in front — so, slower speeds are usable. Top shutter speed is needed when a subject moves straight across at close range (top right panel above).

		↓ OR ↑	↘ OR ↖	→ OR ←
15 FT.		1/200	1/400	1/800*
25 FT.		1/100	1/200	1/400*
50 FT.		1/50	1/100	1/200*

HERE'S HOW IT WORKS WITH OTHER SUBJECTS

Subject	Distance	↓ OR ↑	↘ OR ↖	→ OR ←
Pedestrians, Slow-Moving Animals, Construction Work, Street Activities, Playing Children, Boating	25 feet	1/100	1/200	1/400*
	50 feet	1/50	1/100	1/200*
	100 feet	1/25	1/50	1/100*
Track and Field Sports, Baseball, Skating, Yacht and Horse Races, Motorboats, Surf Diving, Views from Trains	25 feet	1/200	1/400	1/1000*
	50 feet	1/100	1/200	1/400*
	100 feet	1/50	1/100	1/200*
Automobile Races, Motorcycles, Airplanes, Fast Trains	25 feet	1/400	1/1000	
	50 feet	1/200	1/400	1/1000*
	100 feet	1/100	1/200	1/400*

*Or use the "panoram" technique described on Page 172.

seems to move. Twenty-five feet away, as you watch from the curb, it appears to move much faster. And as it comes abreast of you, it zips by with a sudden whoosh — and is gone! A block away, as you view it tail-on, the motion again seems almost zero.

So, we can set up a rule: The more distant the subject . . . the more direct its approach or departure . . . *the slower it moves in relation to your camera.* Look at the table of angles, distances, and shutter speeds (Page 170), and you'll see that there's quite a field left for the moderate-speed camera — *if* you watch the
✦ angles.

speed and angle ▶

Compare these pictures carefully; they further illustrate the table on the facing page. For any such pictures, you'd naturally look ahead, set the lens for the largest opening that would cover the track sharply, and set the shutter for the highest speed the light permitted.

In the top picture, the horses at the left are approaching almost head-on, and those at the right are at about 45 degrees. No horse is very close to the camera. At 1/100 second, with luck, you'd get a picture sharp enough for contact prints; at 1/200, moderate-size enlargements might turn out well; at 1/400, everything would be sharp enough except the feet of the leading horses (which are likely to blur even at 1/1000 second).

In the second picture, the leading horses are almost side-on to the camera. For equivalent sharpness, all the shutter speeds above would have to be doubled—1/200, 1/400, 1/800.

In the bottom picture, all the horses are side-on and really moving. Here's where you want 1/400 or 1/800 — or where you use the "panoram" technique (Page 172). Actually, this picture was risked at 1/250, *f*/4.5, and it's reasonably sharp.

panoraming — the big exception

Normally, you hold your camera still during exposure — or you get a sadly blurred picture. But suppose, as that automobile went by, you had swung the camera in unison with it, keeping the car centered in the finder? In that event, both car and camera would have been standing still in relation to each other — and if you'd released smoothly "in stride," you'd have a sharp picture.

This technique is known as "panoraming." It works beautifully with speeding automobiles, speedboats, and motorcycles; the vehicle stays sharp, but the background streaks out into a mile-a-minute blur, with a terrific effect of speed. Try it on horse races and bike races, too; the legs will be somewhat blurred at low shutter speeds, but that usually adds to the impression of fast action. It also works on ski shots — on either snow or water.

← "Panoraming" is the smart way to overcome shutter limitations. This picture was taken at 1/50 second; the photographer simply moved the camera, keeping the race car centered in the view-finder. The background draws out in a long blur, but the car is sharp. To take such pictures, the subject must be suitable (an automobile or motorcycle is fine, but the horses on Page 171 would have blurred legs) and you must not pause as you trip the shutter.

Picture at right illustrates the basic principle of "panoram" shots. Camera and subject move together, in a fixed relationship. When both are moving at the same rate, neither is moving at all — as far as subject sharpness is concerned. In this shot, of course, the camera was located in the second "plane" back. Note blurred background. ➡

172

are you on good terms with your camera?

Sports photography calls for smooth action and sharp timing. Know your camera thoroughly; it should be easy and familiar in your hands, and every adjustment should be "second nature" with you — because there's no time for fumbling.

Look ahead; try to predict the *probable* opportunities, the *probable* spots where they'll occur, and the *probable* speed of the action. Then you'll be able to choose a logical camera position — and can set your lens, shutter, and focusing in advance. When the right moment comes, you're ready.

viewpoint makes a big difference

A sports shot is no good unless the action is clear and easy to understand. For sports such as football, basketball, and tennis, a high position looking down on the field or court is best when you want general views of the game. But to dramatize a single player, a very *low* position is often better, with the figure silhouetted against the sky.

Don't be afraid, at the proper moment before or after a game, to ask a player to pose for you. Explain the picture idea you have in mind, ask him to help you with it, and he'll usually be tickled pink to serve as your model.

High viewpoint is best for team and field sports (such as baseball) ➡

while low viewpoint, with the camera angled upward, helps dramatize a single figure against the sky. ⬇

shoot plenty — and select the best

Experienced sports photographers know that it's false economy
to be parsimonious with film. They shoot as many pictures as
possible — well aware that the last "extra" shot often turns out
to be the best of all.

And they pay attention to the "sidelights," too — the spectators,
the coach, the line-up, the band, the team coming on the field.
Although not a part of the game itself, these side glances are
needed to provide a well-rounded story of a sporting event.

final step — on the enlarging easel

Because time is precious and action fleeting, the negative of a
sports picture rarely includes just what you want — no more and
no less. In a later chapter, you'll learn about the magical things
that can be done with an enlarger in your darkroom — how unwanted material can be "cropped away" at the top, bottom, or
sides of a picture . . . how the angle can sometimes be changed
for a more exciting and dramatic effect. It's sufficient here to
point out that you need not wait for *perfection* in shooting a
sports picture. There's ample opportunity, later on in the dark-
174   room, to make it perfect — and make it *big*.

← Flash, where permitted, is mighty useful in
picturing night sports. The SM or SF lamps
have a very short flash period — about equal
to a 1/200-second shutter speed — so they
help stop action in dim arenas even with slow,
simple shutters. Hockey shot, below, shows
what you can do with fast lenses, Kodak
Super-XX Film, and existing light. Exposure
was 1/25 second, *f*/3.5, made at the face-off
before players went into action. ↓

Picturing flowers

STEP OUT INTO YOUR FLOWER GARDEN, and select one perfect bloom. Before you pluck it, view it from different positions and at different levels—down low, up high. At each position, observe the form of the flower; consider both its outlines and the angle at which the sun strikes it. Rotate the flower in relation to the sun; you'll find one position in which the pattern of light and shadow best reveals the sculptural form. Observe the background; from some viewpoints it will be spotty and confused. Try placing a plain background of white, black, or tinted cardboard behind the flower, and observe its effect.

You see, picturing a flower is something like making a portrait of a person. In a sense, you're trying to bring out the personality of the flower, as well as obtain an attractive likeness. Snapping the picture is just the last stage; it's the preliminary steps that count—the selection of subject, lighting, viewpoint, camera distance, and background.

there's fascination in it

Whether you work in full color or black-and-white, flower photography provides one of the most fascinating among the many camera specialties. Some enthusiasts concentrate on single blooms . . . others enjoy picturing small groups, or flower arrangements, with occasional pictures of the entire garden or a particularly attractive border or corner.

Your equipment is simple: a camera, one or two Kodak Portra

Lenses, and a Kodak color film (or, a Kodak Wratten K-2 Filter and a Kodak panchromatic film).

Panchromatic film is best for black-and-white shots, because it is sensitive to all colors; on most other films, red flowers tend to record as black, and blue flowers tend to be relatively pale. Use a panchromatic film, with a K-2 Filter over the camera lens, and the black-and-white "tone values" in a group of flowers (or any other brightly colored subject) will appear in a more natural relationship.

For full color, Kodachrome Film or Kodacolor Film is a natural choice. A Kodak Pola-Screen can be used over the camera

← This rose practically offers a "short course" in picturing flowers. It's a close-up — nicely filling the space. The background is plain, and well chosen to contrast with the subject. Camera angle and height (fairly low) were wisely chosen to bring out the form and accent the pride of the flower. Lighting is for dramatic effect, with strong contrast of light and shade — much stronger than you will usually want in a picture of a flower. Enough foliage has been included to provide a "base" that satisfies the eye. The dew on the petals adds a sense of freshness and textural quality. This is an indoor picture, made with photo lights. A small lens opening was used to assure adequate depth of field for crisp detail.

Patterns of flowers are often pictorially worthy. Coleus at top right is interesting for its leaf edging; at right, Cineraria offers a striking pattern with its cerise-and-yellow petals and brown centers. Both these pictures are black-and-white prints from full-color Kodachrome originals.

lens when there is blue sky behind the flower, and you want to record it as a richer blue.

portra lenses for real close-ups

The average camera does not focus for extreme close ranges; but if you set it at "infinity," and put a 3+ Portra Lens over the camera lens, you can bring the camera to just 13 inches from a flower; and if you set the camera for 3½ feet, the taking distance can be only 10 inches! The 2+ Portra Lens provides a range of about 13 to 21 inches, and the 1+ a range of about 20 to 45 inches. (Each lens is supplied with a sheet of exact instructions, distances, and field sizes; don't lose it!)

These handy little lenses make a tremendous difference when you picture a flower or any other small subject—especially if you make pictures in color, for screen projection. Imagine picturing a single rose in close-up, and then showing it in full color, four or five feet wide, on a projection screen!

A simple "focal frame" makes it easy to take flower close-ups; you don't even have to look through the view finder. At top left, a quickly improvised frame for a miniature camera (note Kodak Portra Lens on camera lens). Front of frame comes exactly at the plane of focus of the slip-on lens. Directly above, a more finished focal frame is shown in use; inside of frame is slightly larger than the area covered by the lens. At left, water lily is typical of close-ups that can easily be taken with this device.

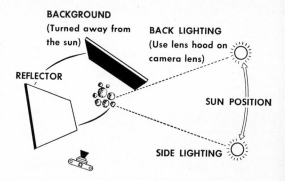

At right, a handy setup for pictures of flowers. Cardboard background blocks out irksome details (compare iris pictures at bottom of page). Reflector helps illuminate shadow side of subject, an important point for good full-color work. Use lens hood on camera when you take back-lighted pictures, so sun won't shine into lens.

BACKGROUND (Turned away from the sun)

BACK LIGHTING (Use lens hood on camera lens)

REFLECTOR

SUN POSITION

SIDE LIGHTING

reflectors for flower portraits

Soft lighting and plain backgrounds are desirable in flower portraits. The wise photographer will equip himself with several sheets of cardboard or thin wood (about the size of a newspaper page) — some white, for reflectors or light backgrounds; some dull black, for dark backgrounds; and some in color, with at least one a rich sky blue. These are used just as the diagram indicates — background behind the flower, and a reflector in front, placed so that it softens the shadows to just the degree desired. Take care to make the shadows light enough — because your film, especially a color film, tends to see them darker than your eye sees them.

Study carefully the illustrations in this chapter; observe how the photographer chose his viewpoint, lighting, background,   **179**

and the pose of each flower. Then start making your own collection of flower pictures; you'll find it both entertaining and rich in its rewards.

Combinations of two Kodak Portra Lenses permit extreme close-ups, such as this of a flowering crab blossom. Note the well-illuminated, delicate shadows on the petals. In a color shot, shadows should usually be barely visible.

The pansies below are backlighted — a type of lighting that lends unusual brilliance and sparkle to a flower picture, especially to a full-color transparency. Transparencies are commonly viewed by projecting them on a screen; perhaps you can imagine this close-up in full color, magnified 6 feet wide and 4 feet high, on your own home screen, for the delight of your friends and guests. ⬇

◄ For color, nothing beats the soft, diffuse lighting of a hazy or cloudy-bright day. Delicate flower hues register more pleasingly, and there are no violent contrasts of light and shade to worry you. On a sunny day, if you want this type of lighting, place a card between the sun and the flower, so that all the light comes from the sky. Then (for color film) put a Kodak Skylight Filter on your camera lens, and give the exposure your Snapshot Kodaguide indicates for "cloudy bright" or "hazy sun"—whichever fits the prevailing light conditions.

To set off blossoms and tall flowers, few outdoor backgrounds can compare with a clear blue sky. Use a low camera position, aiming somewhat upward.
↓

Now
we specialize

You're an all-around picture taker now. You know the basic rules for picturing people, keeping a family record, covering a vacation in pictures, taking sports shots, picturing flowers, snap-shooting after dark, and so on.

Are there other worlds to conquer? Certainly! This chapter touches on three important ones: still-life, "table-top," and trick photography.

imagination time in Lilliput

Slip a Portra Lens on your camera, and bring out the photo lights. Clear a suitable table. Find some salt, cotton, cardboard, scissors and paste or glue, tissue paper, toys — almost any kind. In making table-top pictures, we don't search for subjects; we *create* them.

Start simply. Salt or baking soda make wonderful "snow"; so try a skiing scene. You can easily cut skis from cardboard, to

← Looks quite real — but don't be fooled. It's a "table-top" shot with salt for snow on the ground, and fluffy cotton for the cloud of snow behind the skier.

At right you see the actual setup; even the steep slope is "faked" by clever choice of the camera angle. Photographer is puffing smoke through a tube, for additional realism. →

Imagination and ingenuity — plus the simplest materials. That's what makes a good "table-top" shot. Figures dancing at right are made of pipe cleaners; the orchestra is a black paper cutout. At bottom of page, some spring clothes-pins and soda straws, cleverly lighted, make a squad of soldiers; at bottom right, features painted on a few oranges create opportunity for a charmingly humorous "story-telling" shot. The queer "bug" at top of facing page is merely a pair of eyeglasses; smart lighting does all the rest!

attach to a doll's feet. A bit of carpet makes fine grass; try a simple golf scene. Pebble surface glass or crumpled glassine paper make excellent "water" on which to array tiny sailboats — and the boats are easy to make from paper, cardboard, and toothpicks.

From these, proceed to more ambitious efforts. Make each picture tell a story — comic, dramatic, or purely whimsical. Don't waste time on extreme realism of detail. Use your lights to emphasize the important details of the scene, and throw unimportant details into shadow.

Experiment with materials. Paint features on an egg, glue on legs and arms made of pipe cleaners, and do a "Humpty Dumpty" series. Try a "Jack and the Beanstalk" shot; a scene from "Alice In Wonderland." The sky's the limit, and you can be as clever or fanciful as you like.

As to technique. Support your camera firmly, stop the lens 183

← Table-tops in color, too. They're lots of fun. Don't bother to seek perfect realism; a table-top shot is better if you recognize it as such upon close examination.

Still-life photographs (see below) are worth while either in color or black-and-white. You can learn a great deal about lighting and pictorial arrangement as you group common objects for an interesting or harmonious effect. For this candlelight exposure, 30 seconds, *f*/8, on Kodachrome Film, Type A. ↓

Another charming "table-top" setup. (Don't take the name too literally; some "table-top" shots are best posed on the basement floor, or in the kitchen sink.) The appeal of this one, obviously, comes from the duckling's delighted expression as it greets the spring showers. For extreme close-up pictures such as this, Kodak Portra Lenses are extremely desirable. A Kodak Tourist Camera or Kodak Reflex II Camera, with an adapter kit and miniature film, also enable you to cover small areas. You can also make enlargements utilizing just a part of the negative (see Page 192).

down to a very small opening (you need the extra depth of field in close-ups), focus accurately, and make time exposures. For lighting, you can use either photofloods or ordinary home lights (as outlined in the chapter "Pictures After Dark").

pictorial still-life studies, too

Still-life is akin to table-top photography. But here, the idea is to group interesting objects in a harmonious relationship, achieving beauty in the pattern of shapes, shadows, and textures.

Any grouping may be made to serve; the value of the picture will depend on your skill in arrangement. Try art objects, cut glass, fruit, flowers, and other articles that are attractive in form; 185

"Table-topping" really becomes fun when you start developing story ideas, amusing situations, or human-interest problems for your table-top subjects. Here's an example, and the materials are most simple . . . a toy dog, an enlargement of a puppy picture, and a broken heart cut out of paper. How about a picture of a toy cat, frightened by a magazine illustration of a dog . . . a toy chick, duck, or elephant trying to walk a tightrope . . . a tiny toy elephant startled by a large toy mouse? Start on one idea, and you find it leads to another, then another.

Ghosts in the house? Nothing to it. ➜
Just put your camera on a tripod, and
make one exposure of the frightened
subject. Place the "ghost" in the
scene, and make a second exposure
— not as long as the first. You need
a black background, and the easiest
way to get one is to pose your subjects in front of an open doorway,
with no lights in the room beyond.
Your "live" subject should not move
during the two exposures.

arrange them to please the eye, and then light them in a pleasing
manner. Such work provides wonderful training in pictorial
composition.

stunt pictures and camera trickery

Have you ever photographed a ghost? It's easy — but you must
furnish the ghost yourself. Set up your camera for a time exposure of the room in which the spook is to appear. Make the exposure. Next, without winding the film or moving the camera, let
the "ghost" (a friend or member of your family) enter the scene,
and pose. Make a second exposure, about half as long as the
first. Your picture will show the room, with the ghost as a trans-
lucent figure — you can see right through him!

multiple exposure — face to face with yourself

Set up your camera in front of a wide doorway, leading into an
unlighted room. This provides a black background. Now, stand
in the doorway, left of its center, and shake your fist at the right-
hand space while a friend snaps your picture. Move to the right-
hand side, and shake your fist at the space where you were first

186

◀ Camera on tripod.
Make one exposure;
let subject move to
next chair; make an-
other exposure —
and so on. Put more
light on the subject
than on the table
(because every sta-
tionary object in the
picture receives ALL
the exposures).

← Sure, it's just a "gag" shot — but it would make a wonderful cover for an album of humorous closeups of people. The amazing balancing act (shown at right) is merely a matter of lining up the distant subject's foot with the near subject's hand. Use a small lens opening, for sharpness near and far.

— while your friend snaps a second picture on the same film. Result? — a photograph of you arguing with yourself.

The trick is in the black background. Details of a lighted background would show through you in such a "double-exposed" shot—you'd be *transparent!* Take care, too, that the two poses don't overlap; position marks on the floor may be helpful, or if you're using a camera with ground-glass focusing, the first pose can be traced on the back of the glass as a guide for the second pose.

silhouettes — day or night

Stretch a sheet over a doorway or window, opening to a bright outdoor scene. This will provide a luminous white background. Pose your subject *in profile,* indoors, darken the room, and make a short time exposure. You'll get a silhouette picture — subject black, background white.

To achieve the same effect at night, stretch the sheet over an interior doorway, put a photoflood lamp behind it, place your subject in front of it (see below), and make a short time expo-

187

Superman, at left, is a cut-out figure, pasted on an up-angle shot of a sky-scraper — then copied with a close-up lens. At right, the fisherman was cut out of an enlarge-ment, pasted on card-board, and posed on the lip of the cream pitcher. Such "com-binations" can be quite puzzling to the uninitiated, if you do them carefully.

sure. All lights, of course, must be turned off in the room where camera and subject are located.

Outdoor silhouettes can also be made. The best time is near sunset. Place your subject directly between the camera and the setting sun, so his body will conceal the sun, and make a snap-shot exposure.

pictures in the looking-glass

Mirror pictures are easy — but there's a focusing trick to remem-ber. Pose your subject, and set up the camera so it images the mirror reflection. Close the lens down to a small opening. Now, measure from the camera to the mirror, and from the mirror back to the subject. Set the focus for the total distance (subject-to-mirror-to-camera) and the reflection will be sharp in your picture. Remember, too, that your photo lights should illuminate your *subject*, not the mirror.

Suppose, in this mirror shot, the camera is 5 feet from the mirror, and the boy is 1 foot from the mir-ror. Then the reflection will be 6 feet from the camera. As a practical matter, in most shots, you'd just focus for the distance from camera to mirror — and then use a very small lens opening, to insure ample depth of field. Observe that all the light is on the boy — not on the mirror. →

Light in
the darkroom

Good photofinishing service is available everywhere nowadays, at moderate prices — so, you don't *have* to do your own developing and printing. However, most enthusiasts insist on making their own prints, because of the extra creative opportunities and latitude for individual artistic achievement.

There's only one way to find out if you'll enjoy darkroom work. Get a simple outfit — such as one of the Kodacraft Photo-Lab Outfits — and try it. Complete instructions come with the outfit

1. Mix solutions . . .

2. Check temperature...

3. Line up trays

4. Unroll film . . .

5. Remove paper . . .

6. Wet film fully

7. Develop . . .

8. Rinse in water . . .

9. Fix until clear

Here's a step-by-step picture story of how you develop film and make prints. Detailed instructions come with your Kodacraft Photo-Lab Outfit, and are also in the booklet "Developing, Printing, and Enlarging," at right, available from your Kodak dealer. Kodak Verichrome Film can be developed under a red safelight (steps 4 through 9)— and it's quite a thrill to see the pictures form as you "see-saw" the film back and forth through the developer. Panchromatic films (Kodak Plus-X and Super-XX Film) should be developed in complete darkness; a film tank is best for them. Printing (steps 13 through 16) is done under a yellow safelight; and if you use Kodak Velite Paper, no safelight is needed — ordinary not-too-bright room light is safe with this remarkable paper.

and the operations aren't complicated—even though the picture story which starts on Page 190 may suggest a long pull. Most of the steps are brief; film developed by the "see-saw" method takes only about five minutes, and a print develops in about one minute. You see results in a jiffy.

you can actually see it happen

Make your first negatives on Kodak Verichrome Film, so you can develop them under a red safelight and have the thrill of seeing the pictures actually "come up" on the film. Make your first contact prints on Kodak Velite Paper; it can be comfortably processed in moderate room light, without a safelight.

Prints made with the negative and paper sandwiched snugly together are called "contact prints." Enlarged prints, or "enlargements," are made by projecting light through a negative, 191

Wash fully ...   **11. Sponge and dry ...**   **12. File negatives, or** ▶

how an enlarger works

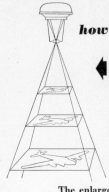

Light from the lamphouse at top is projected through a lens, down to a sheet of highly sensitized paper. The distance from lens to paper determines how much the original image is enlarged. The lamphouse and lens can be moved up and down, until you determine the exact size you prefer.

The enlarger also allows you to select just part of a negative—the best part. At top, right, is a print from an entire negative. Below it, an 8x10-inch "test" enlargement has been made, and two L-shaped rulers or "croppers" are being used to select the best composition for the final enlargement shown on Page 193. With experience, you can "crop" right on the enlarging easel (Page 194, top).

and thence through a lens, onto a sheet of very highly sensitized paper. After the exposure, the enlarging paper is developed and fixed in the same manner as a contact print.

an enlarger "gives you wings"

The great advantage of enlarging is that, even from small

negatives, pictures can be blown up to dramatic and impressive

13. Print, with print frame, contact printer, or in an enlarger (top of p

Compare the enlargement at right with the original picture at top left. With the enlarger, you are able to pick out the real "heart" of the picture, and "blow it up" to any reasonable size. Fine-grain negatives no larger than the small picture below are often enlarged to 11 x 14 inches—and even larger, for home decoration and salon exhibition.

proportions; unwanted material at top, bottom, or sides can be "cropped away," simply by filling the enlarging paper with the part you want to print; and individual portions of the picture 193

DEVELOPER

STOP BATH   DEVELOPER

FIXING BATH

14. Develop print ...   **15. Use stop bath ...**   **16. Fix briefly, and** ▶

This is how the image, projected from your film negative, appears on the enlarger easel. After lining up the image just as you want it, in the size you want, you snap off the enlarger light—then put the sensitized paper in place, and snap on the light again to make the exposure. In this picture, the sensitized paper is in place, and a "dodging paddle" is being used to hold back the light from a portion of the scene that would otherwise print too dark. For a larger picture, the enlarger head is moved higher on the column. On Page 195 are, at left, the budget-priced Kodak Hobbyist Enlarger, and, at right, the famous Kodak Flurolite Enlarger with paper-cabinet base, interchangeable lenses, vernier focusing control, and special distortion control.

can be selectively lightened or darkened by "dodging" (see above), so that the final effect is exactly what you want.

Camera enthusiasts commonly make contact prints for file use, and to determine the exact "cropping" desired in an enlargement; but nearly all serious work is done by enlarging. Prints for salon exhibition are made 11 x 14 inches or larger, on 16 x 20-inch mounts. Almost without exception, the full-page pictures in this book are enlargements from small negatives. If you find that you enjoy darkroom work, you should obtain a good enlarger as soon as possible, and try to set up a permanent working arrangement that will enable you to explore the full creative possibilities of print-making. Either of the enlargers

194

17. Wash fully ...

18. Dry in blotter roll ...

19. Put in album, or .

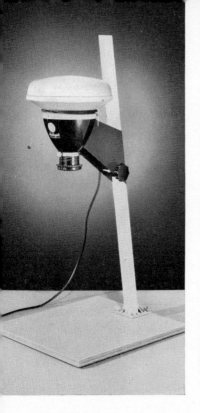

pictured above — the budget-priced Kodak Hobbyist Enlarger, or the superb Kodak Flurolite Enlarger — will serve you well.

When you first start making enlargements, select a moderate size — 5 x 7 or 8 x 10 inches — and get several paper contrasts. Kodabromide Paper E or G, in contrasts 1, 2, and 3, is recommended for its ease of manipulation. Practice making many moderate-sized enlargements until your darkroom technique is fully developed; and then you can progress safely to the dramatic exhibition sizes — 11 x 14, 14 x 17, and 16 x 20 inches.

make the darkroom simple but adequate

Since you will certainly want to make big prints as soon as you have learned the ropes, equip yourself at the start with trays of generous size. Your darkroom setup need not be elabo-

0. Study for outstanding enlargement possibilities.

rate — but it should be adequate to your needs. If possible, partition off a portion of the basement, and install an L-shaped or U-shaped counter, about like a kitchen sink counter, with a large flat-rim sink. Partitions of wallboard on lightweight wood frames are satisfactory — just so they exclude all light. The basic floor plan shown below is only 6 x 8 feet, and this can be reduced to 5 x 7 feet if necessary.

basic equipment—and plenty of paper

In addition to your enlarger and print trays, you must have one over-the-sink safelight. A large safelight at ceiling level adds greatly to your comfort. You will already have a measuring graduate and thermometer from your beginner's outfit. Use Kodak prepared chemicals, and you avoid mixing complicated formulas. Reserve for later purchase such luxuries as a Kodak Utility Footswitch (it frees both your hands for "dodging") and a Kodak Automatic Tray Siphon to speed up print washing. Then, at the start, you'll have more to spend on printing paper — so you can make more prints, larger prints, and fully develop the skills and satisfactions darkroom work offers you.

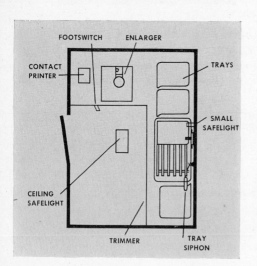

FOOTSWITCH   ENLARGER

CONTACT
PRINTER

TRAYS

SMALL
SAFELIGHT

CEILING
SAFELIGHT

TRIMMER

TRAY
SIPHON

Thousands of amateur photographers do excellent darkroom work at night in the kitchen or bath — but a compact, permanent setup is better. The L-shaped counter in this 6x8 darkroom is about 36 inches high, about 24 wide. Cover it with linoleum for a waterproof working surface. Use a flat-rim sink, with a frame of 1-inch wood slats in the bottom to support your trays. Keep equipment such as the print trimmer, blotter rolls, and extra trays, under the counter. Provide a wall shelf for chemicals and paper. If possible, put an electric outlet in each wall. A dry basement is the best location in most homes.

196

To get the most

out of your pictures

TAKING PICTURES IS FUN . . . making enlargements is fun . . . but the true value of photography lies in the *use* you make of your pictures. That's why this chapter on the uses and applications of pictures was saved until last. It is perhaps the most important chapter in the entire book.

Very few amateur photographers derive all the possible value from their pictures. Most of them maintain an album — in a sort of hit-and-miss fashion — without ever discovering how good a really well-planned album can be. The still wider uses — in picture books, in gift books for special occasions, gift enlargements, enlargements for home decoration, projection slides for home entertainments, records of family projects, pictorial records related to other hobbies or collections, photographic bookmarks, greeting cards and announcements, exhibitions and salons, camera club competitions and prize contests, and many other potential uses — are all too often overlooked.

albums—the family's pictorial history

A family picture album is not one book, but a series that grows with the years. Properly planned, properly kept, these books can become the most treasured of possessions.

There are two ways to arrange such an album series. One is a straight chronological plan, with each picture inserted as soon as a print is ready, and a caption or notes placed underneath. The other is a classified plan — a separate book for the general family history, a book for each member of the family, and additional books for special occasions — vacations, Christmas pictures, and so on.

contact albums—and enlargement books

A third variation, preferred by many amateurs who have enlarging equipment, combines these two plans. As pictures are made, contact prints go into the chronological albums. Then, from time to time, the best pictures on a particular theme are selected and made into a book of impressive enlargements.

Opportunities for such special books are innumerable. Each vacation, Christmas, Thanksgiving, birthday party, Halloween party, anniversary celebration . . . the baby's first year (and each

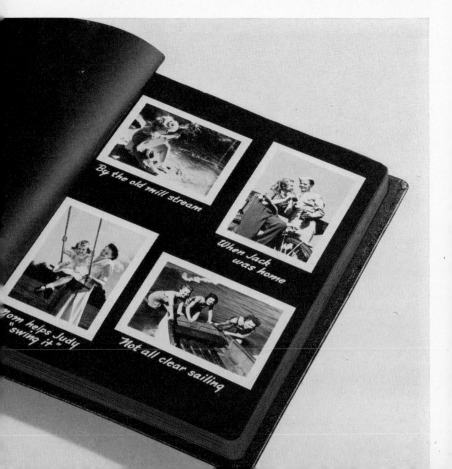

Here's a gold mine — hundreds of snapshots, accumulated through many years, all carefully placed in albums by month and year. Such a collection is priceless, a true family history. But for real enjoyment, you want to go one step farther, and gather the best pictures in handsome enlargement books, as illustrated on Pages 202, 203, 206, 207, 212, and 213. With your own enlarger, it's easy — and such books yield satisfaction far beyond their relatively small cost.

succeeding year, for that matter) . . . Junior's sports, from his first bag of marbles to his college football letter . . . Betty's picture story of her first high-school year . . . the life of a favorite family pet . . . and so on. Pick up a pencil, and you can list twenty others in five minutes.

titles to tease your imagination

Just run through a few titles, and visualize the books. "Mother's   199

Hats — 1928 to Now." "Places We Have Lived." "When I Was Six." "Bobby Gets A Bike." "We Went To Washington." "Grandmother's Farm." "They Named Me Rover." "As Jane Grew Up." The great thing about all such books is that they increase in value and interest as the years pass. They become, quite literally, priceless.

Well, time's a-wasting. The pictures you can take today will grow into picture books as good as any of these. Different, perhaps — but just as thoroughly worth while.

keep negatives safe, neatly filed

The most valuable part of your picture collection is the original negatives. Select a negative file — such as the Kodak Negative File — before you pick an album. And, as pictures are made, file and index each negative with care.

For the general album, choose a sturdy, standard type — one of good capacity, and preferably one to which leaves can be added. Take each group of prints, arrange them neatly on the page, and attach them in a permanent manner. Under each one, place the essential information you will always want to have available — such as the date, the place, the occasion, identifying names, and other notes of interest. No need to explain what is in the picture; if it is a good picture, it will explain itself.

From time to time, go through the album for picture-book themes — and when you find one, start an enlargement book. It

200

Carefully file the original negatives of all your good pictures. Beware of using ordinary paper envelopes, for some papers contain sulphur compounds that stain negatives. The best system is to use a regular Kodak Negative File, which has an individual transparent envelope for each negative or strip of miniature negatives, and an index for quickly locating any negative you want. Write the file number alongside each picture in your contact-print album, and you have a perfect system.

Color enlargements, too

Your original Kodacolor Print or Kodachrome transparency is merely a beginning—you have just started to realize the potentialities. From the Kodacolor negative, beautiful full-color enlargements can be made, for gifts, for home decoration. Prints in a wide range of sizes can also be made from Kodachrome transparencies—some of the proper size for a pocket case, others large enough for framing or gift presentations. Enlarged transparencies are readily available from miniature Kodachrome transparencies; and at very small cost you can have duplicate transparencies, mounted as 2x2-inch slides just like the original, to exchange with other camera fans. Ask your Kodak dealer for full details.

These handsome enlargement books are 11x14 inches. See Page 203 for details.

need not be completed all at once, but can grow as the general collection produces more pictures that fit in.

enlargement books for gifts

When a gift occasion approaches — involving someone who is closely linked to you by sentimental ties — your picture collection becomes a treasure chest. Consider the value, to a parent, of a picture book devoted to the children or the grandchildren, tracing highlights of the years. Consider, on a wedding anniversary,

The impressive football album and New York vacation album, on facing page, and the wedding album on this page, are produced simply by enlarging from small negatives (you've already seen the original pictures, in the original snapshot size, earlier in this book). These books are 11x14 inches; the $2\frac{1}{4}$ x $2\frac{1}{4}$ contact print, next to the New York album, gives you an index of their size. To produce such an enlargement book, you simply make enlargements of the pictures you want included, preferably on double-weight enlarging paper. Full sheets are used; if a picture does not exactly fit the page format, you mask off the undesired portion, leaving a wide white margin (as on Pages 212 and 213). Pictures can be mounted back to back with Kodak Thermount Tissue or Kodak Rapid Mounting Cement, to make rigid pages; or they can be arranged unmounted in facing pairs, which give you two blank pages following each two pages of pictures.

To make a title in white block letters, as on the football album, you can cut the letters out of black paper or cardboard, and place them on the enlarging paper before you make the exposure. They should, of course, appear in a dark portion of the picture. Another method is to letter in white on a large black card, and then photograph the card; this gives you a negative which can be sandwiched with the picture negative when you make the enlargement. A third method (good for either white or black lettering) is to make an enlargement, mount it on cardboard for flatness, do the lettering on it, and then photograph it; the final print for your book cover is made from your "copy negative." There are other methods which you will pick up quickly when you begin to do darkroom work. You can also letter with drawing ink directly on the cover print, and then cement a sheet of transparent acetate over it, or have a heavy acetate sheet bound with the rest of the book as a protective front cover. Plastic or wire spiral binding is relatively inexpensive, and many printers and binders now offer it.

For home entertainments

Full-color transparencies are treasures to be enjoyed by the whole family, and to be shared with friends, guests, and visiting kinsfolk. A Kodaslide Projector enables you to bring your slides to life on the screen—to bring back colorful vacation spots and family experiences with so much sparkle and realism that you're carried right back to the place and the day! Group your slides carefully, in a natural story sequence or by type of subject, and you can present a show that has all the poise and smoothness of a finished theatrical production. Your Kodak dealer will help you select the Kodaslide Projector and slide filing equipment that exactly fits your needs. For small groups, a Kodaslide Table Viewer (pictured on Page 56) is the ideal device.

In emergencies, a ready camera can have great value—whether it's loaded with color film or black-and-white. Aside from its dramatic wort a picture such as this may contribute materially to the investigation the fire's origin, and may also be helpful in connection with insuran adjustment. There are many other situations in which a camera all load and ready for action can ably serve you.

Community events (above) are frequently colorful, and are best pictured on color film. Incidentally, black-and-white negatives and prints can be made from any Kodachrome transparency, and black-and-white prints of good quality are made directly from any good Kodacolor negative.) If you are a collector, color film may also have special uses and applications for you. ➡

Remember this picture, from the chapter "Pictures Right Around Home," early in this book? It's a grand shot in any size — but here, as the front cover of a big book of baby enlargements, it becomes tops. This could be the first volume in the pictorial history of your own baby, the start of a long series (see facing page).

the delight of a gift book which looks back to the beginning — revisiting remembered places, recreating good times and significant occasions out of the past.

On such occasions, even a single picture, attractively enlarged and mounted suitably for framing, makes a welcome gift. The

Baby books don't really need titles or volume numbers — because the changes in the child establish the sequence very nicely. These two books could be, let's say, Volumes 4 and 5 of the baby history that starts on the facing page. It's important, at the start of such a series, to decide on a uniform size and style of binding, so all the books will match as the "picture history" grows. And here's another hint — remember Grandmother and Grandfather, and make *two* prints of the most outstanding pictures. Then, when a gift occasion comes around, you'll have the extra prints all ready to bind as a gift book. No need to tell you how much more such a book means to fond grandparents! Individual gift pictures, too, can be printed at the same time you make prints for your own personal enlargement books.

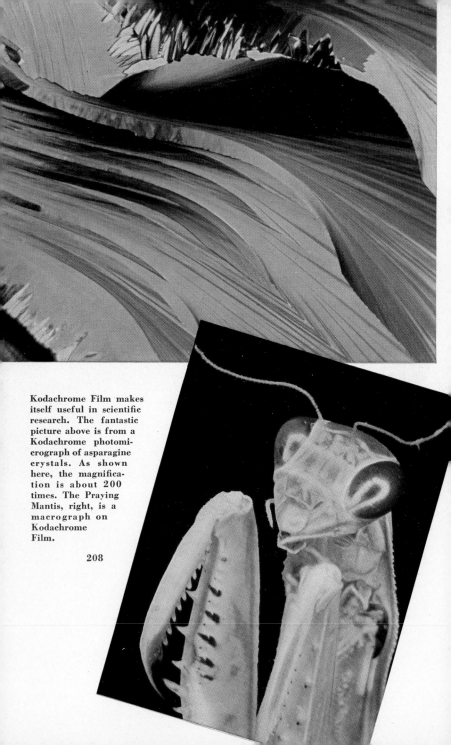

Kodachrome Film makes itself useful in scientific research. The fantastic picture above is from a Kodachrome photomicrograph of asparagine crystals. As shown here, the magnification is about 200 times. The Praying Mantis, right, is a macrograph on Kodachrome Film.

208

picture book, containing a dozen or more enlargements, simply multiplies the pleasure manyfold.

let snapshots accompany your letters

There's another, more casual, use of snapshots that's too often overlooked. When you write to family friends or kin, enclose a few of the family's latest snapshots with each letter. Extra prints for this purpose are inexpensive and well worth while; and almost every reply will comment on the pictures with lively appreciation.

home decoration—and photomurals

Framed enlargements from your own photographs—particularly scenics, flower studies, and pictures of family activity — can contribute greatly to home decoration. Scenics have a particular place in living room, library, study, and entry hall. If the library or study reflects certain interests, you probably have, or will have, photographs related to the same interests, and worthy of exhibition there. Enlargements of sports shots often find proper place in a den or recreation room, as do pictures of family activities.

Some of these enlargements will be black-and-white; others should be full color, made from your own Kodachrome transparencies or Kodacolor negatives. Eventually, you may be mak- **209**

It's a pleasant habit to include snapshots with your letters—and it saves a lot of explanatory writing, because a good photograph tells so much more than words do. When you order contact prints, or make them yourself, keep your friends and relatives in mind, and provide for extra prints. This also applies when you're shooting Kodachrome Film — just take two shots of the scenes you'd like to share. The extra original costs somewhat less than a duplicate made later — and the lightweight cardboard slides mail easily in a letter.

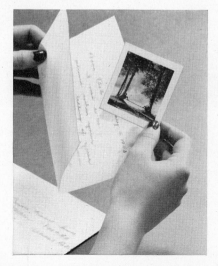

Attractive "panoramic" photomurals such as the one on facing page are easily
made with your own enlarger. You simply take a series of pictures as described
on Pages 114-115, allowing for a slight overlap where each meets the next. All
should be taken at the same lens opening, shutter speed, and camera location;
and developed at the same time. Then enlargements should be made on paper
from one package, and developed for the same time in the same developer, to
assure good matching. Trim and frame them as shown — and there you are!

ing your own full-color prints; in the interim, you can always order Kodachrome Prints or Kodacolor Prints made for you.

Photomurals—huge enlargements several feet high and wide, mounted as part of the wall—are growing in popularity. There are probably several places in your own home where pictures from your own collection might be so used. Photomurals of reasonable size can be made by any amateur photographer who has enlarging equipment and a basic knowledge of darkroom work; they may be made on one large sheet of photo paper, or several smaller sheets matched and mounted together.

The handsome photomural opposite is 40 inches by 8 feet, and all in one piece. Sheldon Hine, Fort Wayne, Ind., made it while still an amateur photographer (he's now a professional). Such prints are too ambitious for a beginner—but an experienced amateur, or studio which does photomurals, can make them from any sharply detailed, fine-grain negative of reasonable size.

Hine used a 4x5-inch negative, and Kodak Opal Paper (which, like other Kodak enlarging papers, can be had in rolls 41 inches by 10 or 30 feet, as well as sheet sizes). Size and placement of the picture were carefully thought out in advance, as it is the dominant feature of the room. For better composition, Hine "flopped" the negative (reversed it left to right in the enlarger) to make the distant vista come at the right-hand side of the scene.

Developing "troughs" were made of regular house guttering, painted with chemical-resistant plastic paint. One contained the developer, another a stop bath, and a third the fixing bath. Hine and his wife stood on stools, with the trays between them on the basement floor, and "see-sawed" the paper back and forth just as a film is developed (see Page 190). A smooth hardwood dowel, floated in each trough, helped hold the paper under; and anti-fogging agent in the developer prevented aerial fog. After washing and drying, the big print was mounted on tempered wallboard, with carpenter's glue.

Probably the most convenient paper to use for these prints is Kodak Resisto Rapid N; its water-resistant base speeds up washing. Kodak Dektol Developer diluted 1-to-4 for slow development, and with Kodak Anti-Fog added, is correct. Test exposures should be made very carefully, because the big sheet of paper represents an investment of several dollars; and the whole operation of developing should be rehearsed before you put the actual print through.   211

photo "pin-up boards" for boy or girl

Junior members of the family who have their own rooms are usually eager for an individual scheme of decoration. Favorite
family pictures, enlarged and framed, make prized possessions.
In addition, a photographic "pin-up board," for current snapshots of friends and schoolmates, is a welcome feature.

More and more juniors, these days, are operating their own
cameras — and, it must be said, are often taking pictures that put
their elders' work to shame. The more fortunate are members of
school camera clubs, with access to excellent enlarging equipment. As a result, they are able not only to pursue a wholesome
and constructive hobby, but also can decorate their rooms with
their own creative work — as happy a combination as any parent
could wish.

when guests come to your house

212 Everybody enjoys good pictures — and guests will enjoy yours if

you present them in the right manner, either as a picture collection, or as pictures projected on a screen.

Right here, however, let's have a heart-to-heart talk about "album manners." Possibly you have had somebody back you into a corner, hold a snapshot album under your nose, and turn the pages (at the rate of about two each hour) while he gave you a running discourse on the who, what, when, where, why, and how of each picture. In a very short time (approximately at once) you were very sick of Aunt Minnie, and wanted to go home.

Don't show your prints that way. Indeed, you should rarely bring out the general album. Show your guests the special books of enlargements we discussed above. Let the guest hold the book **213**

Special themes produce fine enlargement books. On facing page, a spread from a book about a child and her pets; below, one from a Christmas book.

These two spreads show how you can accommodate various shapes of pictures to the book. Each picture should be "cropped" for best appearance. Deep white margins lend smartness. The original size doesn't matter; enlarging can always fill the page.

and turn the pages himself. Omit the commentary; a good picture doesn't require explanation, and comment won't help a bad one. Adhere to these restrictions (no matter how it hurts) and your guest will enjoy your pictures; he'll probably go home thinking you're one whale of a good photographer.

organizing the slide show

Slide shows should be organized with the same consideration for your guests. Eliminate the less interesting shots ahead of time. Arrange the remaining ones in natural groups; that is, don't scramble a group of ski shots together with a series of flower shots. Next, arrange each group into a pleasing *sequence* — and you're all set to go.

If possible, set up the screen before your guests arrive. Check the projector lamp to be sure it's all right (it's always wise to have a spare lamp on hand), and be sure the connecting cord is untangled. Decide where the projector is to be, and what you'll put it on. Decide also how your guests will be seated (a carpeted floor is a comfortable spot, and it saves arranging chairs).

In short, be ready to start the show promptly — and to carry it through with a minimum of commentary. Your guests will enjoy it that way, and so will you.

photography and other hobbies

One of the most pleasant features of photography is the manner in which it aids and complements most other hobbies.

If you collect glass — or mineral specimens, or old guns, or

almost any other type of small object — your camera with a close-up lens can provide pictures to exchange with other collectors.

If you collect documents, your camera — again with a close-up lens — provides a copying means, enabling you to make facsimile records of each valuable item, so that the original need not be handled.

If you're a student of nature, your camera — with a close-up lens, and loaded with full-color film — enables you to picture specimens in their natural habitat before you bring them home.

If you're a model builder, your camera permits you to retain a complete pictorial record showing each step in the construction — a record that doubles the pleasure you derive from the completed model.

photography and special occasions

Your camera enables you to bring home a full story of almost any event you attend . . . the dog, horse, or livestock show in which you have an entry . . . the model aircraft meet in which one of your models competes . . . the garden tour, Chamber of Commerce tour, political convention or business convention you attend. In fact, there are few phases of human activity in which the camera cannot serve as a friendly companion — and the best of all possible notebooks.

Many hobbies can become "collecting" hobbies *only* with the aid of a camera. If you're interested in bridges, old buildings, railroading, aircraft types — the camera is the only means whereby you can bring home what you see precisely as you see it. This 215

Photography fits in with any other hobby — and it assists them all. Nature subjects (far left), model making, railway trains — no matter what hobby you follow, your camera can broaden it, make it more interesting, and preserve a permanent record of all the details you want to keep. No wonder there are so many millions of cameras in active use!

holds true even if you're skilled at drawing or painting; and it's a fact that many good artists now carry cameras, loaded with full-color film, to supplement their sketchbooks.

If you're still in school, the camera can help you illustrate term papers and laboratory projects; too, it provides a means whereby you can record your student activities and associations, creating a "personal yearbook" of your own.

the camera and family projects

When the family builds a new home, a day-to-day picture record is well worth while — and sometimes may have an outstanding value if there is any dispute about any phase of the construction.

Landscaping operations should be recorded in "before" and "after" pictures.

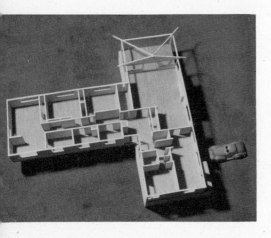

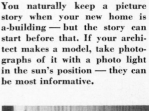

You naturally keep a picture story when your new home is a-building — but the story can start before that. If your architect makes a model, take photographs of it with a photo light in the sun's position — they can be most informative.

Also, take exterior views, selecting the viewpoint from which you'll see the completed house . . .

. . . Then paste a snapshot cutout on drawing paper, sketch in various landscape treatments, and you can more accurately decide just what plantings you prefer.

one snapshot, but

...Look how it grows, as the maker's ingenuity finds additional uses and applications for it. At right is the original picture — a snap of nodding wheat, with sky and landscape beyond. It's a purely decorative type of picture, not startling or disturbing, but pleasant to view — the kind of picture you can live with, and that fits in almost anywhere. So ...

← The first application is a mounted print, used as a home decoration. It is not permanently framed here, but is arranged for easy interchange with other prints. Next, just below, it has been trick-printed into an attractive symmetrical design (you merely make one print, then turn the negative over and make a second print — which comes out reversed left-to-right). The two prints are then trimmed and mounted edge-to-edge. ↓

The symmetrical plan at right can be made into a frieze pattern (by adding other left-and-right prints), or multiplied as shown below, where it has become an interesting decorative design for a serving tray. It's all done by trimming and matching prints. ↓

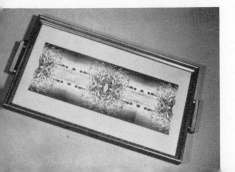

Finally, a straight enlargement has been utilized as a shade for a wall fixture (at right); and the maker of this picture will probably find other uses in the future. Just shows you what imagination can do!

Here's more decorative trick printing. Above, a straight shot of some wood planings, against a dark background. It's an interesting picture alone; and by combining left-and-right prints with negative prints, it becomes an attractive wall design. The two negative prints are simply contact-printed from the two positive prints — exactly as a contact print is made from a film negative. Clever, isn't it? ➡

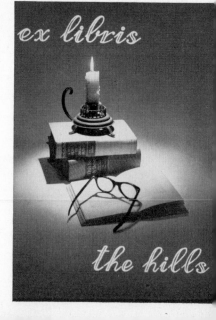

ex libris

the hills

Above, a photographic book end; at right, a neat photographic book plate.

Many a businessman utilizes the personal camera as a sort of memorandum book – to note down business ideas, his store and window displays, store signs, methods of doing a particular operation, and so on. Such note-taking is quick, handy, and often repays its small cost many times over.

special uses for photography

Christmas comes every year – and experience has proved that the most individual Christmas card is a photographic card. Any amateur photographer can print Christmas cards from one of his own negatives – or can have a photofinisher do it at small cost, comparable to that of routine printed cards. For many other occasions – notably births and engagements – photographic announcements offer unique advantages.

Photographic bookmarks are also a growing vogue. They are printed – from one of your own pictures – in the same manner as photo-greeting cards. And they offer the same characteristic individuality.

clubs, exhibitions, and contests

Every camera enthusiast should join a camera club. If there's none in your neighborhood, maybe you can interest other camera fans and organize one. But it's better to join a strong club, already in operation, than start a new one.

Camera club membership gives you companionship in your hobby, the spur of competition, and the advantage of friendly, expert advice. Most clubs have print competitions and special photo projects; some of the largest ones sponsor print salons which enable you to put your work into competition with fine 219

Opportunities for novel photographic greetings and announcements are many — at Christmas, anniversaries, and (see right) when a new member joins the family. This is simply a paste-up of newspaper headline letters to make the announcement message. It was photographed and contact prints sent out.

prints from camera fans all over the United States—or the world. Even if you're not a club member, you should eventually submit prints to salons; an acceptance is proof that your work is good in the eyes of independent experts.

Leading salons — and prize competitions, some with extremely tempting prizes — are listed in the photographic magazines. You will do well to subscribe to one or more of these magazines. They bring you examples of good photography, helpful photographic information, ideas, and news of what's going on in amateur photography. Some of them operate their own contests — and regularly publish winning pictures. So do many newspapers.

photography as a profession

Many young people today are attracted to photography as a profession. For these, encouragement plus a word of caution is in order. It is true that the field of professional photography is growing, and that each year there are new opportunities in press and illustrative photography, in scientific and industrial photographic work, and in portrait and general commercial studio work. Success in any of these fields, however, is not to be had by wishing; it calls for a measure of native ability, plus either thorough schooling in a good photographic school or the equivalent in hard, routine studio work — without the immediate glamour that many expect. As in other fields, there is always room at the top for those of outstanding ability and serious intent, and the rewards are high; but for the careless worker and the second-rater, there is no room anywhere.

220

Index and Glossary of Photo Terms

Numerical references below are page numbers. In addition to the terms in this basic glossary, many specialized chemical and optical terms are used in advanced photography; these will be found defined in photographic dictionaries and reference texts.

position of related or non-conflicting colors (58-59).

Composition—Arrangement of the material in the picture space. In color (58, 59, 65). Landscape and general (27, 111, 114, 115).

Contact print—A print the same size as the negative, made by placing the negative in contact with sensitized paper, and exposing to light (192).

Contrast—The range from white to black in a monochrome print; from clear to maximum density in a negative; from lightest to darkest point in a scene; and, in color, the range from pale to deep plus the opposition of "warm" and "cool" colors. A print or negative is said to be *flat* (too low in contrast), *soft* (moderate contrast), *full scale* (full range from white to black), *snappy* or *brilliant* (clear whites and deep, rich blacks), *hard* or *harsh* (too contrasty, with loss of detail).

Correct exposure. See *Exposure*.

Crop—To eliminate part of a picture, by trimming a print, or in enlarging (192-195), in order to improve the composition or exclude undesired material (16, 17, 21).

Darkroom—A room (from which all outside light can be excluded) fitted for photographic developing and printing (189).

Development—The conversion to a visible image of the latent image (37) on an exposed film or plate, or sensitized paper, by immersion in a suitable chemical bath or "developer" (190-191).

Depth of Field—Distance between the nearest and farthest points sharply defined by a lens. This varies both in size and location as the lens aperture and focus setting are changed (45). Focusing guide (77).

Diaphragm. See *Iris Diaphragm.*

Dodging—Selective screening of the light image projected on the enlarger easel, to make selected areas of the print lighter or darker (194).

Double exposure—Two pictures taken on one film, either through carelessness (10) or for a deliberate purpose (186).

Element—A single lens, one unit of a camera lens system. See *Lens.*

Elevation—Height at which camera is placed in relation to height of subject (7, 71, 73, 97).

Emphasis—Accenting a particular point in a picture, by use of lines, contrasting light and dark masses, or other devices (15, 25, 31).

Enlarger—A device consisting of a light source, negative holder, lens, and means for adjusting these so as to project an image from a negative to a sheet of sensitized paper; by this method, prints much larger than the original negative are made (192-195).

Enlargement—A print larger than the negative. See *Enlarger.* Uses for enlargements (202-213).

Equipment, selection of (39)

Exposure—This term is loosely used in many meanings, such as: *a.* Act of tripping the camera shutter, so that the film is *exposed* to light; *b.* The lens aperture and shutter time used in taking a picture; *c.* The total amount of light which reaches the film (this is controlled by the strength of the light, the lens aperture, and the exposure time). "Correct exposure" takes place when the aperture, time, and light are correct for the film (52, 56) or printing paper (34, 191, 192).

Exposure tables (52, 59, 160)

F-System—A system for marking lens speeds and apertures (42, 43).

Family Events (123)

Filter—A device of dyed gelatin, gelatin sandwiched in glass, or colored glass; it is placed over the camera lens and filters out certain colors of light (50).

Filter factor—A multiplying number used in calculating correct exposure when a filter is used (51).

Film—An emulsion of gelatin and light-sensitive silver salts coated on a flexible transparent base (33).

Fine-Grain film—Film in which, after development, the silver particles forming the image are small and fairly uniform in spacing; such films permit enlargements of greater size with better image texture (49).

Fireplace pictures (80)

Fireworks pictures (165)

Flash, photoflash—Photoflash lamps (154) are commonly used in situations where natural light is inadequate for pictures. These lamps are used in reflector-type holders, and the flash is generally synchronized with the opening of the camera shutter (46, 47). Flash exposure guidance (79, 155, 160).

Flasholder, Kodak—A battery-and-reflector unit for flash photography; used with flash-synchronizing Kodak cameras and others having standard ASA bayonet connectors (50).

Flat lighting—Lighting with little or no contrast of light and shade.

Flat print (See *Contrast*)

Floodlighted buildings (165)

Flop—In making prints or enlargements, to turn the negative face-up, so that the scene will print in reverse left to right (211).

Flower pictures—Basic techniques (175); equipment and films (175, 176); close-up aids (178); reflectors and backgrounds (179).

Focal Frame (178)

Focal Length (42)

Focus—Adjustment of camera lens or camera-to-subject range so the subject is sharply imaged (36, 45). "Out of focus," "in focus," "sharp focus," are phrases commonly encountered.

Fog—An over-all graying of a negative or print, usually caused by exposure to unsafe light, or by too much manipulation in air during development, or by overdevelopment, or by age of the film or paper, or storage in a warm or humid place.

Foreground—The area between the camera and subject (31, 111). "Foreground object," "foreground figure" — a person or object deliberately included in order to provide a nearby frame or vista for more distant material.

Garden pictures (73)

Gradation—The tonal transition from light to dark in a negative or print. Photography tends to excel all other art processes in delicacy of tonal gradation.

Ground-Glass focusing (46)

Highlights—The brightest areas of a subject or print (darkest areas of a negative).

Holiday pictures (123)

Horizon—The earth or water line at the limit of vision. An ocean or prairie horizon will usually tend to fall exactly on the mid-line of a picture; tip the camera up or down to avoid such "bisection" (28, 29).

Interior views (77, 78, 161)

In the Country—Picture planning (106); campfires (110); landscapes (111); atmosphere (113); lighting and composition (113); farm activities (117); animals (117); winter (118).

Iris diaphragm—Device for adjusting lens aperture (36, 37, 44). Consists of thin metal blades which "open up" or "close down" as the adjusting ring or lever is manipulated.

Key—The range of tones employed in a picture. If the picture consists primarily of light, delicate tones, it is "high key"; if primarily dark, heavy tones, it is "low key."

Kitchen pictures (82)

Kodachrome Film (54)

Kodacolor Film (53)

Kodak Portra Lenses—These are positive lenses which slip over the camera lens, shortening its focal length and thus permitting pictures of small objects at closer-than-normal range (50).

Kodaslide — Miniature Kodachrome transparencies are normally returned after processing in the form of mounted 2x2-inch slides, or Kodaslide Transparencies, ready for use in a Kodaslide Table Viewer or Kodaslide Projector (56, 57).

Lens—A disk of optical glass or other transparent material, ground concave or convex, and thus able to focus rays of light. The lens of a fine camera is made up of several elements of selected optical glass, and is properly called a "lens system" or "objec-

tive" (33, 36, 42-43). See also *Positive Lens.*

Lens cleaner, lens tissue (11, 38)

Light—Radiant energy to which the eye is sensitive. Photographic materials are also sensitive to the ultraviolet rays, and in some cases to the infrared rays, adjoining the visible spectrum (34).

Lighting—The illumination on a subject; particularly the arrangement of such illumination. See also *Back Lighting, Flat Lighting.*

Living Room pictures (77)

Location—The spot where a picture is taken; more specifically, where the subject is located (6).

Merger—Juxtaposition of a subject and a background object of about the same tone, so that they "merge" in the picture (30).

Miniature camera—A camera which accepts small films, usually 35mm or 828; usage generally restricts the term to well-made cameras equipped with relatively fast, highly corrected lenses (48, 49).

Mirror pictures (188)

Moonlight pictures (114, 162)

Multiple exposures (186)

Negative—A photographic record, usually on film, in which the tone values of the subject are reversed (black is white, etc.). In a color negative (53) each color of the subject is represented by its complementary color. See also *Positive, Print, Paper Negative.*

Night, outdoors (162)

Nursery, pictures in (74, 75)

Open Shade (70)

Orthochromatic film—Film which is sensitive to all visible light except red (49).

Overexposure (10)

Panoram—To move the camera in synchronism with a fast-moving subject (26, 170).

Panorama—A broad view, usually scenic; a print of such a view, made by joining prints from two or more negatives (114, 210-211).

Paper negative—A negative print, printed from a positive print, and used to produce a final positive. Because retouching and alterations are easy on the first print and the paper negative, this roundabout procedure is often employed in making exhibition prints.

Parade pictures (30, 97)

People, pictures of—Naturalness (147); lighting (149); backgrounds (150); using flash (151); camera elevation and angle (152).

Photoflood—Photoflood lamps are inexpensive incandescents of high actinic (photographic) efficiency, especially suited for indoor snapshots with fast panchromatic films (74, 75, 76, 80, 82, 154, 155). Exposure table (160).

Photo-Greeting—A greeting card (Christmas, anniversary, etc.) produced by photographic methods, usually contact printing, and usually incorporating a personal snapshot (219).

Photography—The recording of images by the action of light (33).

Photomural—A large photographic print, usually planned as the main feature of a room wall, and usually permanently mounted on the wall (209-211).

Photon—A quantum of light radiation (36).

Planning pictures (106, 107, 123, 126).

Portrait—A photograph of a person, an individual likeness (16).

Positive—A picture or photographic print in which tone values of the subject appear in normal relationship (white objects appear white, shadows are dark, etc.); all prints from *negatives* (which see) are positives.

Positive lens—A convex lens which will form an image of an object on a flat surface.

Print—A picture, usually on paper, and usually produced from a negative on film or paper (but sometimes from a positive on film or paper). See *Contact Print, Enlargement*.

Projector—A device for showing lantern slides and transparencies on a screen (56, 57).

Range—Distance from camera to subject. Range finder (45).

Record picture—One primarily intended to show sharp, clear, legible detail (30).

Reflector—Any device used to reflect light onto a subject (55, 59, 62, 70).

Reflex camera (46, 47)

Safelight lamp—An enclosed lamp, fitted with a filter to screen out rays to which film or paper is sensitive (190). See also *Fog*.

Salon—A photographic exhibition, usually sponsored by a camera club (219-220), presenting outstanding prints or transparencies.

Seasonal pictures (83, 84)

Series—Several pictures which tell a connected story (8, 9, 142, 143). A *sequence* is a short series with no change of location (140, 141).

Shutter—A mechanical device, part of any complete camera, which covers the lens opening except during exposure (37, 44).

Silhouettes (187)

Silver—Precious metal, essential ingredient of photographic film and paper (33, 37).

Slide—A photographic transparency mounted for projection. See *Projector, Kodaslide*.

Snapshot—A picture taken with a brief or so-called "instantaneous" exposure (as distinguished from a *time exposure*, which see). Also applied to pictures taken casually or with brief preparation, not meticulously planned for artistic effect or to convey an idea.

Soft—Low or moderate in contrast. Soft lighting (55) is generally preferable for color photography. A soft print or negative has detail both in shadows and bright areas. See also *Contrast*.

Speed—In reference to film, "speed" means sensitivity to light; a "fast" film is highly sensitive (49). In a lens, speed refers to relative aperture (42-43). In a camera shutter, speed refers to the time between opening and closing; a "fast" shutter permits very brief exposures (44).

Sports pictures—After dark (165); finding opportunities (167); choosing best moment (169); best angle (169); shutter speeds and distances (170, 171); "panoram" technique (172); camera manipulation (173); best viewpoint (173); enlarging (174).

Still-Life studies (185)

Stop—To halt action in a picture (14, 26, 170). Lens *stop*, n., synonym for *aperture*, as "stop $f/5.6$."

Story—The essential idea, action, or situation a picture conveys. A good picture always has "something to tell" (8, 9, 17, 20, 24, 25, 140, 142).

Street activity (95)

Street Scenes, night (162)

Stunt pictures (186)

Subject—The essential material in a picture.

Sunsets, exposure for (63)

Synchronized flash (46, 47, 79, 154, 155). Exposure table (160).

Table-Top pictures (182)

Technique—Correct manner of doing something. Basic picture-taking technique (5); darkroom (190); color (55); child pictures (135); flowers (175); sports (167); after dark (153).

Texture—The surface characteristic that distinguishes one material from another (fur from wood or metal, etc.).

Theater pictures (165)

Third dimension—The feeling of depth, distance, or sculptural quality in a picture (31).

Time exposure—An exposure made by setting the shutter on "T," and pressing the release once to open, once to close (32). Set on "B," the shutter remains open as long as the release is depressed. On "I" or marked fractions of a second, the shutter closes automatically after opening.

Tone—Degree of lightness or darkness in any given area of a print; also called "tone value" or "value." Also applied to the color of an image; brown or brown-black is "warm tone"; bluish or cool black is "cool tone."

Tripod—A folding three-legged camera support (51).

Underexposure (10)

Vacation pictures (123)

Zoo pictures (90, 92)